GLOBETROTTER™
Travel Atlas

SOUTH AFRICA

NEW
HOLLAND

New Holland Publishers (UK) Ltd
London • Cape Town • Sydney • Auckland

First edition   1994
Second impression   1995
Third impression   1996
Fourth impression   1997
Second edition   1997
Second impression   1998
Third impression   2000
Third edition   2001
Fourth edition   2003
Fifth edition   2005
Sixth edition   2006

10 9 8 7 6 5 4 3 2 1

website: www.newhollandpublishers.com

Garfield House, 86 Edgware Road
London W2 2EA
United Kingdom

80 McKenzie Street
Cape Town 8001
South Africa

14 Aquatic Drive
Frenchs Forest, NSW 2086
Australia

218 Lake Road
Northcote, Auckland
New Zealand

Distributed in the USA by
The Globe Pequot Press, Connecticut

ISBN 1 84537 379 0

Publishing Manager: Thea Grobbelaar
DTP Cartographic Manager: Genené Hart
Editors: Alicha van Reenen, Melany McCallum, Tarryn Berry
Designer: Nicole Bannister
Cartographers: Nicole Bannister, Genené Hart
Compiler/Verifier: Denielle Lategan, Elaine Fick
Proofreader: Thea Grobbelaar

Reproduction by Hirt & Carter, Cape Town
Printed and bound by Times Offset (M) Sdn. Bhd., Malaysia.

Cover: *Popular curio markets cater for every tourist's need en route to Llandudno, Western Cape.*
Title Page: *The Wilderness coastline, part of the well-known Garden Route.*

Photographic Credits:
Herman Potgieter, page 33; IOA/Shaen Adey,
pages 49, 59; IOA/CLB, page 24; IOA/Roger de la
Harpe, pages 30, 67; IOA/Gerhard Dreyer, title
page, page 40; IOA/Walter Knirr, pages 10, 16,
18, 54, 70 (bottom), 72, 80; IOA/Peter Pickford,
page 74; IOA/Erhardt Thiel, pages 46, 48, 50;
IOA/Hein von Hörsten, cover, pages 35, 39, 62;
IOA/Lanz von Hörsten, pages 20, 42, 45, 78;
IOA/Keith Young, pages 26, 28, 57, 61, 70 (top).

[IOA: Images of Africa; CLB: Colour Library]

Although every effort has been made to ensure that
this atlas is up to date and current at time of going
to print, the Publisher accepts no responsibility or
liability for any loss, injury or inconvenience
incurred by readers or travellers using this atlas.

Emergency Telephone Numbers
Notrufnummern
Appels d'Urgence

Police	
Polizeirevier	1-0111
Poste de police	
Telephone enquiries	
Telefon Auskunft	1-023
Information téléphonique	
Ambulance	
Krankenwagen	1-0177
Ambulances	

Below: *This brightly coloured South African flag was
first raised at midnight on 26 April 1994. For most South
Africans it is a symbol of hope, uniting the nation in its
effort to reconciliate and become a truly democratic
society.*

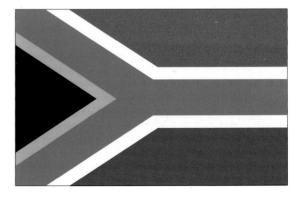

CONTENTS

TOURIST AREAS

MAIN MAP SECTION

INDEX

For ease of use, the Index has been divided into two sections:

• the first focuses on the Tourist Area Maps and related text and photographs.

• the second deals with the Main Map Section only, facilitating the easy location of cities, towns and villages.

National Route Planner

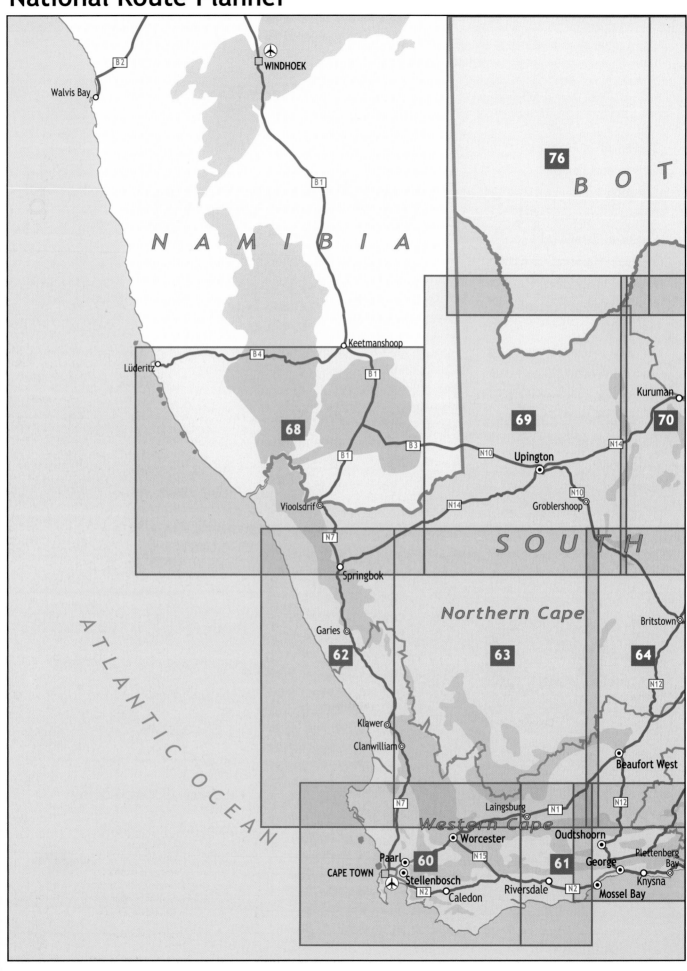

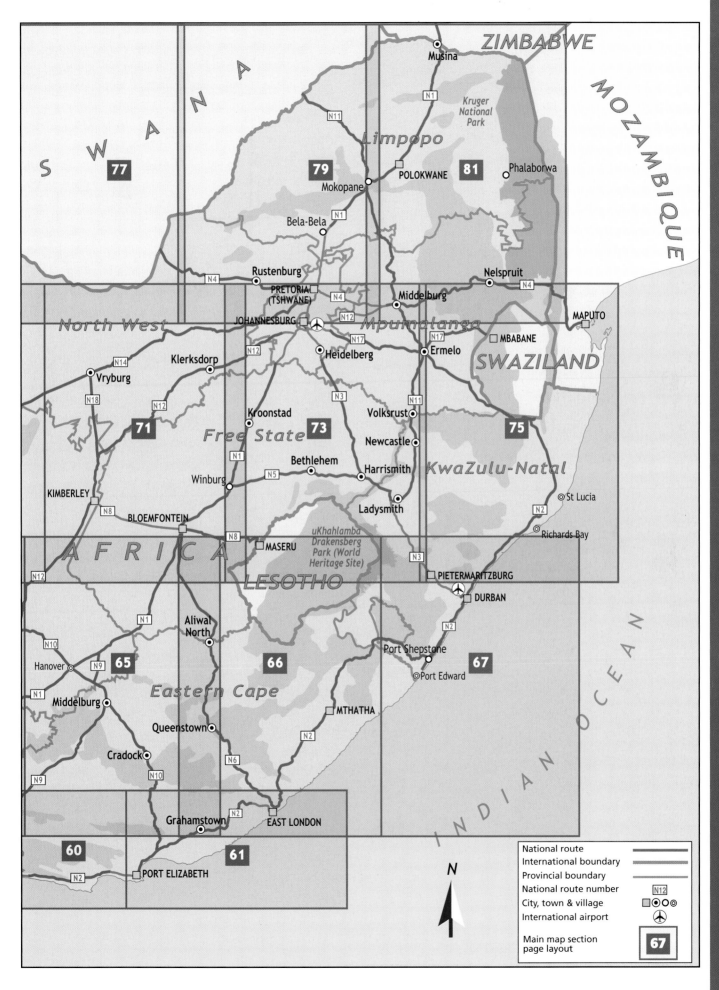

Tourist Area Planner

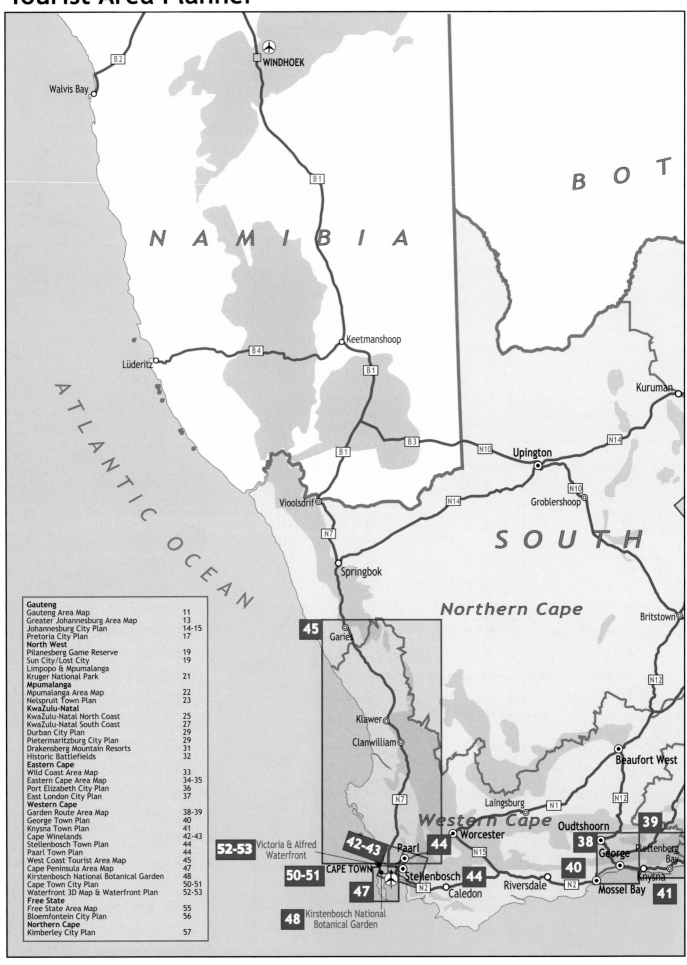

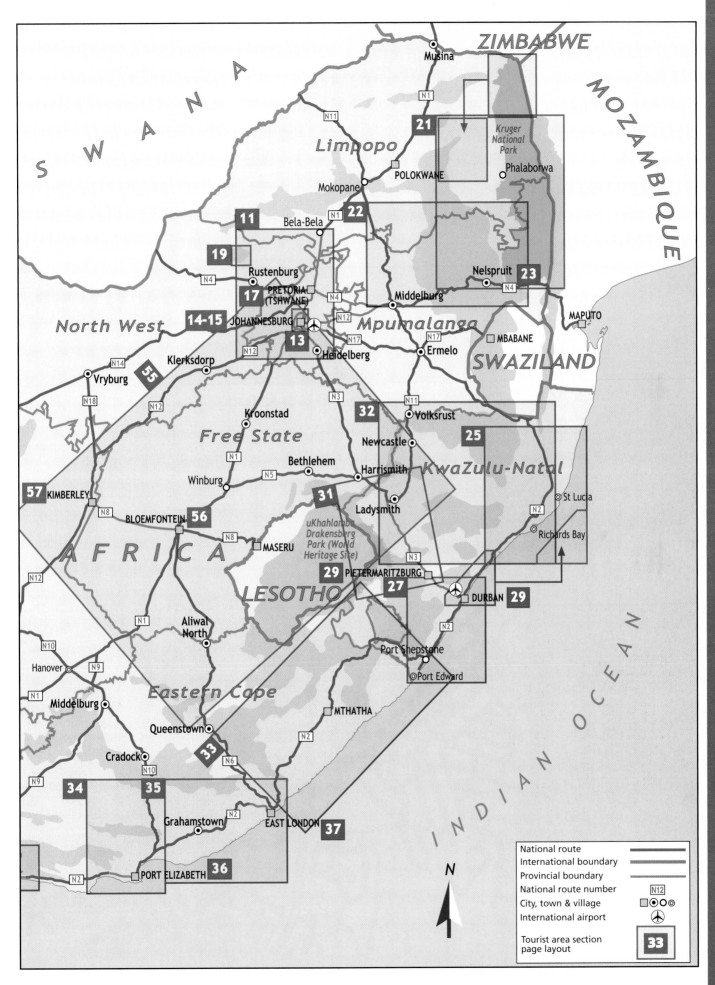

National route	
International boundary	
Provincial boundary	
National route number	N12
City, town & village	
International airport	
Tourist area section page layout	33

Distance Chart

APPROXIMATE DISTANCES IN KILOMETRES	BLOEMFONTEIN	CAPE TOWN	DURBAN	EAST LONDON	GABORONE	GRAHAMSTOWN	JOHANNESBURG	KIMBERLEY	MAPUTO	MASERU	MBABANE	PORT ELIZABETH	PRETORIA	WELKOM	WINDHOEK
BEAUFORT WEST	544	460	1178	605	1042	492	942	504	1349	609	1129	501	1000	697	1629
BLOEMFONTEIN		1004	634	584	622	601	398	177	897	157	677	677	456	153	1593
BRITSTOWN	398	710	1032	609	791	496	725	253	1289	555	1075	572	783	551	1378
CAPE TOWN	1004		1753	1099	1501	899	1402	962	1900	1160	1680	769	1460	1156	1500
COLESBERG	226	778	860	488	848	375	624	292	1123	383	903	451	682	379	1573
DE AAR	346	762	980	557	843	444	744	305	1243	503	1023	520	802	499	1430
DURBAN	634	1753		674	979	854	578	811	625	590	562	984	646	564	2227
EAST LONDON	584	1079	674		1206	180	982	780	1301	630	1238	310	1040	737	1987
GABORONE	622	1501	979	1206		1223	358	538	957	702	719	1299	350	479	1735
GEORGE	773	438	1319	645	1361	465	1171	762	1670	913	1450	335	1229	926	1887
GRAAFF-REINET	424	787	942	395	1012	282	822	490	1321	599	1101	291	880	577	1697
GRAHAMSTOWN	601	899	854	180	1223		999	667	1478	692	1418	130	1057	754	1856
HARRISMITH	328	1331	306	822	673	929	282	505	649	284	468	1068	332	258	1921
JOHANNESBURG	398	1402	578	982	358	999		472	599	438	361	1075	58	258	1801
KEETMANSHOOP	1088	995	1722	1482	1230	1351	1296	911	1895	1245	1657	1445	1354	1205	505
KIMBERLEY	177	962	811	780	538	667	472		1071	334	833	743	530	294	1416
KLERKSDORP	288	1271	645	872	334	889	164	308	763	368	525	1009	222	145	1693
KROONSTAD	211	1214	537	795	442	812	187	339	742	247	522	888	245	71	1724
LADYSMITH	410	1413	236	752	755	932	356	587	567	366	386	1062	422	340	2008
MAFIKENG	464	1343	821	1048	158	1065	287	380	886	544	648	1141	294	321	1577
MAPUTO	897	1900	625	1301	957	1478	599	1071		853	223	1609	583	813	2400
MASERU	157	1160	590	630	702	692	438	334	853		633	822	488	249	1750
MBABANE	677	1680	562	1238	719	1418	361	833	223	633		1548	372	451	2162
MTHATHA	570	1314	439	235	1192	415	869	747	1064	616	1003	545	928	718	2066
MUSINA	928	1932	1118	1512	696	1529	530	1002	725	960	808	1605	472	788	2331
NELSPRUIT	757	1762	707	1226	672	1358	355	827	244	713	173	1434	322	639	2156
OUDTSHOORN	743	506	1294	704	1241	532	1141	703	1705	959	1417	394	1199	896	1828
PIETERMARITZBURG	555	1674	79	595	900	775	509	732	706	511	640	905	567	485	2148
POLOKWANE	717	1721	907	1301	485	1318	319	791	605	749	515		261	577	2120
PORT ELIZABETH	677	769	984	310	1299	130	1075	743	1609	822	1548	1394		830	1950
PRETORIA	456	1460	646	1040	350	1057	58	530	583	488	372	1133		316	1859
QUEENSTOWN	377	1069	676	207	999	269	775	554	1302	423	1240	399	833	525	1829
UPINGTON	588	894	1222	982	730	851	796	411	1395	745	1157	945	854	669	1005
WELKOM	153	1156	564	737	479	754	258	294	813	249	451	830	316		1679
WINDHOEK	1593	1500	2227	1987	1735	1856	1801	1416	2400	1750	2162	1950	1859	1679	

Strip Route

Strip Routes

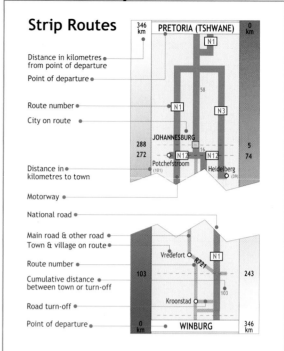

Distance in kilometres from point of departure
Point of departure
Route number
City on route
Distance in kilometres to town
Motorway
National road
Main road & other road
Town & village on route
Route number
Cumulative distance between town or turn-off
Road turn-off
Point of departure

Strip Routes

Strip routes are located throughout the atlas to indicate the distances between major centres in a specific region. Distances between other towns and villages along the route are also shown.

Distance Charts

In order to calculate the distance between two of the country's major centres, locate the name of the first town or city on the vertical or horizontal column on the chart (see above), then locate the name of the other on the second column and read off the number where the vertical and horizontal columns intersect.

Toll Road Chart

Various South African provinces are served by time-saving toll roads. The chart (right) identifies the names of these toll roads, the locations of the toll plazas, points between which the toll roads stretch, and grid references for locating these roads on the maps in this book.

Toll Roads

ROUTE	PROVINCE	NAME	TOLL PLAZA	LOCATION
N1	Western Cape	HUGUENOT TUNNEL	HUGUENOT	DU TOITSKLOOF
N1	Free State	KROONVAAL	VAAL	UNCLE CHARLIES-KROONSTAD
N1	Gauteng		GRASMERE	JHB-VANDERBIJLPARK
N1	Limpopo	KRANSKOP	KRANSKOP	BELA-BELA-MIDDELFONTEIN
N2	Western Cape	TSITSIKAMMA	TSITSIKAMMA	THE CRAGS AND STORMS RIVER
N2	KwaZulu-Natal	SOUTH COAST	ORIBI	SOUTHBROOM-MARBURG
N2	KwaZulu-Natal		IZOTSHA	SOUTHBROOM-MARBURG
N2	KwaZulu-Natal	NORTH COAST	TONGAAT	UMDLOTI-BALLITO
N2	KwaZulu-Natal		UMVOTI	SHAKASKRAAL/STANGER
N2	KwaZulu-Natal		MTUNZINI	MTUNZINI/FELIXTON
N3	Free State	HIGHVELD	WILGE	VILLIERS-WARDEN
N3	KwaZulu-Natal	MIDLANDS	TUGELA	KEEVERSFONTEIN-FRERE
N3	KwaZulu-Natal		MOOI RIVER	FRERE-CEDARA
N3	KwaZulu-Natal	MARIANNHILL	MARIANNHILL	ASSAGAY-PINETOWN
N4	Gauteng	MAGALIES	QUAGGA	PRETORIA-ATTERIDGEVILLE
N4	Gauteng		PELINDABA	ATTERIDGEVILLE-PELINDABA
N17	Gauteng	WITWATERSRAND	DALPARK	SPRINGS-DALPARK
N17	Gauteng		DENNE ROAD	SPRINGS-DALPARK
N17	Gauteng		GOSFORTH	DALPARK-RAND AIRPORT

Climate Chart

Climate Charts

These occur throughout the atlas, and give the average temperatures and rainfall for the relevant region or city.

JOHANNESBURG	J	F	M	A	M	J	J	A	S	O	N	D
AV. TEMP. °C	20	20	18	16	13	10	10	13	16	18	18	19
AV. TEMP. °F	68	68	64	61	55	50	50	55	61	64	64	66
DAILY SUN hrs	8	8	8	8	9	9	9	10	9	9	8	8
RAINFALL mm	131	95	81	55	19	7	6	6	26	72	114	106
RAINFALL in	5.5	4	3.5	2.5	0.7	0.3	0.2	0.2	1	3	4.5	4.5

PRETORIA	J	F	M	A	M	J	J	A	S	O	N	D
AV. TEMP. °C	23	22	21	18	15	11	12	14	18	20	21	22
AV. TEMP. °F	73	72	70	64	59	52	54	57	64	68	70	73
DAILY SUN hrs	9	8	8	8	9	9	9	9	10	10	9	9
RAINFALL mm	152	76	80	57	14	3	3	6	21	67	101	105
RAINFALL in	6	3	3.5	2.5	0.6	0.1	0.1	0.2	0.8	3	4	4.5

BLOEMFONTEIN	J	F	M	A	M	J	J	A	S	O	N	D
AV. TEMP. °C	23	21	19	15	11	7	7	10	14	19	20	22
AV. TEMP. °F	73	70	66	59	52	45	45	50	57	63	66	72
DAILY SUN hrs	10	9	9	9	9	9	9	9	10	10	10	10
RAINFALL mm	91	99	74	58	21	12	9	14	19	42	59	62
RAINFALL in	4	4	3	2.5	0.8	0.5	0.3	0.6	0.7	2	2.5	2.5

DURBAN	J	F	M	A	M	J	J	A	S	O	N	D
AV. TEMP. °C	24	25	24	22	19	17	16	17	19	20	22	23
AV. TEMP. °F	75	77	75	72	66	63	61	63	66	68	72	73
DAILY SUN hrs	6	7	7	7	7	7	7	7	6	5	5	6
RAINFALL mm	135	114	124	87	64	26	44	58	65	89	104	108
RAINFALL in	5.5	4.5	5	3.5	3	1	2	2.5	3	4	4.5	4.5
SEA TEMP. °C	24	25	24	23	21	20	19	19	20	21	22	23
SEA TEMP. °F	75	77	75	73	70	68	66	66	68	70	72	73

EAST LONDON	J	F	M	A	M	J	J	A	S	O	N	D
AV. TEMP. °C	22	22	21	19	18	16	16	16	17	18	19	21
AV. TEMP. °F	72	72	70	66	64	61	61	61	63	64	66	70
DAILY SUN hrs	7	7	7	7	7	7	8	7	7	7	7	8
RAINFALL mm	74	95	106	80	55	40	51	75	93	95	90	74
RAINFALL in	3	4	4.5	3.5	2.5	2	2.5	3	4	4	4	3.5
SEA TEMP. °C	19	19	19	18	18	17	17	17	17	18	18	18
SEA TEMP. °F	66	66	66	64	64	63	63	63	63	64	64	64

PORT ELIZABETH	J	F	M	A	M	J	J	A	S	O	N	D
AV. TEMP. °C	21	21	20	18	16	14	14	14	15	17	18	20
AV. TEMP. °F	70	70	68	64	61	57	57	57	59	63	64	68
DAILY SUN hrs	9	8	7	7	7	7	7	8	7	8	9	7
RAINFALL mm	41	39	55	57	68	61	54	75	70	59	49	34
RAINFALL in	2	2	2.5	2.5	3	2.5	2.5	3	3	2.5	2	1.5
SEA TEMP. °C	21	21	20	19	17	16	16	16	17	18	19	21
SEA TEMP. °F	70	70	68	66	63	61	61	61	63	64	66	70

MOSSEL BAY	J	F	M	A	M	J	J	A	S	O	N	D
AV. TEMP. °C	21	21	20	18	17	16	15	15	16	17	18	20
AV. TEMP. °F	70	70	68	64	63	61	59	59	61	63	64	68
DAILY SUN hrs	7	7	7	7	7	7	7	7	7	7	7	7
RAINFALL mm	28	31	36	40	37	31	32	36	39	38	34	28
RAINFALL in	1	1	1.5	2	1.5	1	1	1.5	2	1.5	1.5	1
SEA TEMP. °C	22	22	20	19	18	16	16	16	17	19	20	21
SEA TEMP. °F	72	72	68	66	64	61	61	61	63	66	68	70

CAPE TOWN	J	F	M	A	M	J	J	A	S	O	N	D
AV. TEMP. °C	21	21	20	17	15	13	12	13	14	16	18	20
AV. TEMP. °F	70	70	68	63	59	55	54	55	57	61	64	68
DAILY SUN hrs	11	10	9	7	6	6	6	7	8	9	10	11
RAINFALL mm	14	17	19	39	74	92	70	75	39	37	15	17
RAINFALL in	0.6	0.7	0.7	2	3	4	3	3	2	1.5	0.6	0.7
SEA TEMP. °C	15	14	13	13	12	12	12	13	13	14	14	14
SEA TEMP. °F	59	57	55	55	54	54	54	55	55	57	57	57

LANGEBAAN	J	F	M	A	M	J	J	A	S	O	N	D
AV. TEMP. °C	17	17	17	16	15	14	13	13	14	15	16	17
AV. TEMP. °F	63	63	63	61	59	57	55	55	57	59	61	63
DAILY SUN hrs	7	6	7	7	8	8	8	7	6	7	7	7
RAINFALL mm	3	2	6	15	20	21	22	18	11	8	4	5
RAINFALL in	0.1	0	0.2	0.6	0.8	0.8	0.9	0.7	0.4	0.3	0.1	0.2
SEA TEMP. °C	15	14	13	13	12	12	12	13	13	14	14	14
SEA TEMP. °F	59	57	55	55	54	54	54	55	55	57	57	57

Legend

Motorway / Autobahn / Autoroute

National road / Nationalstraße / Route principale

Principal road / Regionalstraße / Route principale

Main roads / Hauptstraße / Route principale — Tarred   Untarred

Minor roads / Nebenstraße / Route secondaire — Tarred   Untarred

Route number / Routennummer / Numéro de route — N4   R28   R518

Distance in kilometres / Entfernung in Kilometern / Distance en kilomètres — 19   15

Railway and station / Eisenbahn und Bahnhof / Chemin de fer et gare

International boundary / Internationale Grenze / Frontière internationale

Provincial boundary / Provinzgrenze / Frontière provinciale

Province name / Provinzname / Nom de la province — *KwaZulu-Natal*

Scenic route / Panoramastraße / Route touristique

Mountain pass / Gebirgspaß / Col — *Du Toitskloof*

Motorway & interchange / Autobahn und -kreuz / Autoroute avec échangeur

National reserves and parks / Nationalreservat und Park / Réserve naturelle et parc — *Mountain Zebra NP*

Airport / Flughäfen / Aéroport — INT.   Other

Golf course / Golfplatz / Terrain de golf

Major petrol stop / Große Tankstelle / Station-service

Place of interest / Sehenswürdigkeit / Endroit à visiter — ★ *Historic Houses*

Peak in metres / Höhe in Metern / Altitude (en mètres) — Table Mtn ▲ 1140 m

Mountain range / Gebirgskette / Chaîne de montagnes

Water / Gewässer / Eau — River   Waterfall   Swamp   Dam

Toll road / Mautstraße / Route à péage — Ⓣ

City / Großstadt / Grande ville — ▪

Major town / Kreisstadt / Ville importante — ◉

Small town / Kleinstadt / Grand village — ○

Large village / Größere Ortschaft / Grand village — ◎

Village / Dorf / Village — ○

Lighthouse / Leuchtturm / Phare

Border post / Grenzübergang / Frontière — Lebombo

Cave/Ruin / Höhle/Ruine / Grotte/Ruines

Hotel (selected) / Hotel (Auswahl) / Hôtel (sélectionné) — Ⓗ ALBANY

Picnic site / Piekniekplatz / Pique nique

Safe bathing beach / Badestrand / Baignade autorisée

Viewpoint / Aussichtspunkt / Point de vue

Camp / Camp / Camp — ⌂

Battle site / Hist. Schlachtfeld / Lieu de bataille historique — ✕ uLundi

Caravan park / Wohnwagenpark / Camping pour caravanes

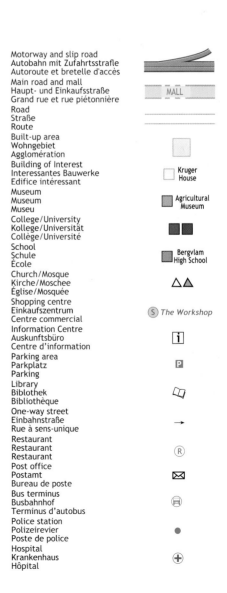

Motorway and slip road / Autobahn mit Zufahrtstraße / Autoroute et bretelle d'accès

Main road and mall / Haupt- und Einkaufsstraße / Grand rue et rue piétonnière — MALL

Road / Straße / Route

Built-up area / Wohngebiet / Agglomération

Building of Interest / Interessantes Bauwerke / Edifice intéressant — Kruger House

Museum / Museum / Museu — Agricultural Museum

College/University / Kollege/Universität / Collège/Université

School / Schule / École — Bergvlam High School

Church/Mosque / Kirche/Moschee / Église/Mosquée — △△

Shopping centre / Einkaufszentrum / Centre commercial — Ⓢ The Workshop

Information Centre / Auskunftsbüro / Centre d'information — ℹ

Parking area / Parkplatz / Parking — Ⓟ

Library / Bibliothek / Bibliothèque

One-way street / Einbahnstraße / Rue à sens-unique — →

Restaurant / Restaurant / Restaurant — Ⓡ

Post office / Postamt / Bureau de poste — ✉

Bus terminus / Busbahnhof / Terminus d'autobus

Police station / Polizeirevier / Poste de police — •

Hospital / Krankenhaus / Hôpital — ⊕

Gauteng

Johannesburg, bustling financial capital of Gauteng and South Africa's largest metropolis, and stately Pretoria, the country's administrative capital, are located 56km (35 miles) apart on the Highveld, the highest part of the great interior plateau. Southwest of central Johannesburg sprawls the urban conglomerate of Soweto, largest of the country's former 'African townships'; farther south is a concentration of industrial centres that includes Vereeniging and Vanderbijlpark, while to the north lie Johannesburg's affluent garden suburbs. All these form what is known as Gauteng — South Africa's pulsating economic heartland.

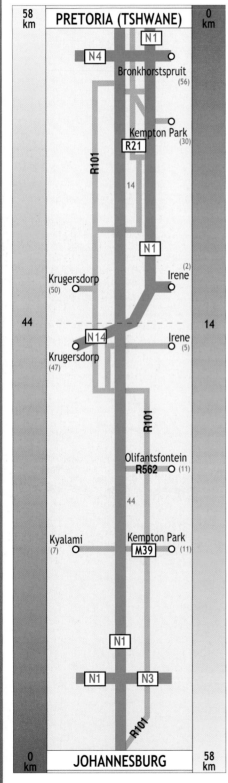

MAIN ATTRACTIONS

Johannesburg: South Africa's commercial and financial capital, a modern city dominated by concrete-and-glass giants (*see* page 12).
Pretoria: the lovely 'Jacaranda City' with a wealth of historic buildings; in October its avenues are strewn with lilac blossoms (*see* page 16).
Sterkfontein Caves: source of artefacts from the dawn of humankind, now a World Heritage Site.

Hartbeespoort Dam: picturesquely situated at the foothills of the Magaliesberg mountain range; popular with many anglers, campers and water-sports enthusiasts.
Casino Entertainment complexes: glittering venues, with much to offer besides gambling, include Sun City Resort and Casino Complex, Carnival City, Caesar's, Montecasino, Gold Reef City and the Carousel.

USEFUL CONTACTS

Police, tel: 1-0111 (national number).
Ambulance, tel: 1-0177 (national number).
Johannesburg General Hospital, tel: (011) 488-4911, fax: 643-1612.
Johannesburg Metropolitan Tourism Association, tel: (011) 327-2000, fax: 327-7000; tourist information.
Computicket, tel: (011) 340-8000.
First National Bank, tel: 0800 110 132.
AA of South Africa, tel: 083 843 22.
South African Tourism, tel: (011) 895-3000.
Gauteng Tourism Authority, tel: (011) 832-2780, fax: 832-2781.

Below: *Designed in grandiose style, the Gold Reef City casino complex in Johannesburg contains a casino, retail outlets and a four-star hotel.*

TRAVEL TIPS

A network of well-signposted roads and highways links the centres in this region. Speed limits apply to usual urban zones like schools and hospitals. As in crowded city areas worldwide, crime presents a growing problem. Common sense, however, goes a long way towards preventing potentially unpleasant situations. Below are some safety guidelines:
• Plan your itinerary before setting out.
• Don't leave your vehicle if it is bumped from behind, but rather proceed to a populated and well-lit area.
• Never park in poorly lit areas.
• Don't walk around alone after dusk.
• Leave your personal belongings and valuables safely stored in the hotel when you venture out.

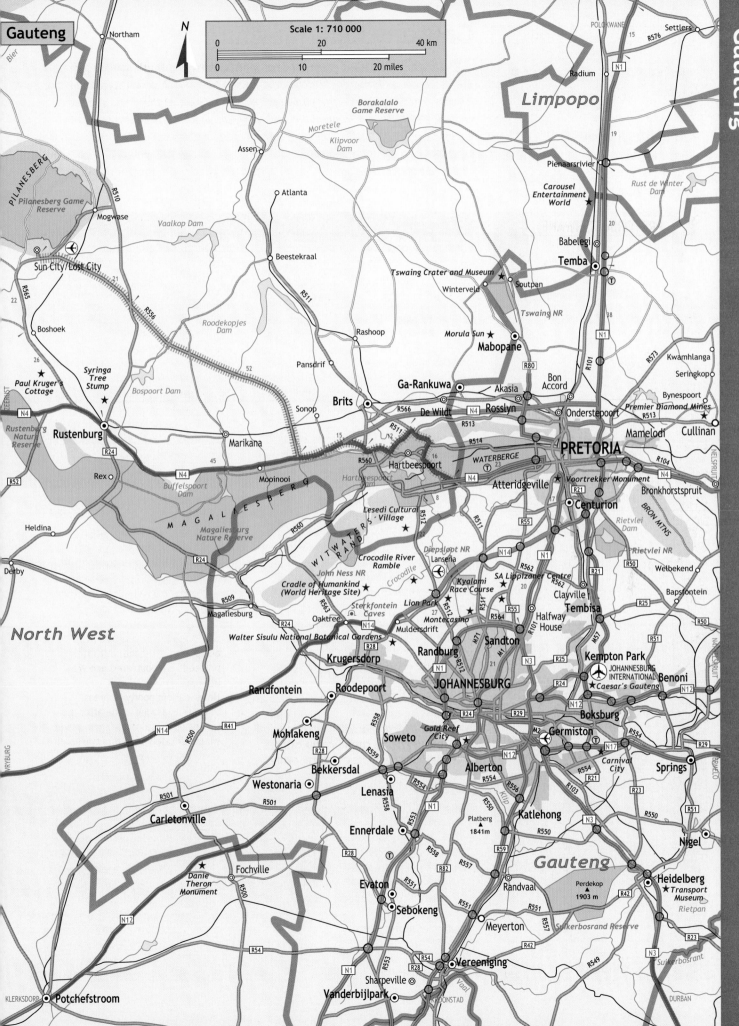

Greater Johannesburg

The huge, yellow mine dumps and rusting headgear of the abandoned gold mines to the south of modern Johannesburg are evocative reminders of the days when the city was essentially a diggers' camp — a visit to Gold Reef City lets you relive the exciting gold-rush past. To the north, wealthy garden suburbs like Sandton and Randburg offer upmarket shopping centres, fashionable boutiques, souvenir shops, an impressive range of cosmopolitan and ethnic restaurants, and numerous entertainment venues. Informal art and craft markets are regularly held in the many parks. For the golfer, there are a dozen challenging courses.

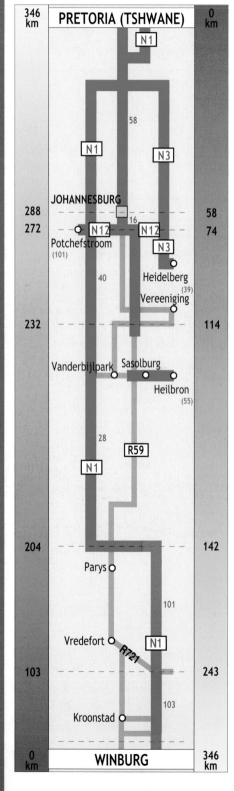

MAIN ATTRACTIONS

Gold Reef City: experience Johannesburg during the gold-rush days. Descend deep into a mine, visit the museums and the fairground, tel: (011) 248-6800.

Brightwater Commons: attractive complex with live entertainment, restaurants, shops and pubs.

Market Theatre complex: theatre and jazz venue in the city centre, and the location of Newtown Art Gallery, tel: (011) 832-1641.

MuseuMAfrica: displays and artefacts illustrate South Africa's turbulent history from prehistory to the present, tel: (011) 833-5624.

Flea markets: the Johannesburg (at the Market Theatre) and Bruma Lake flea markets offer almost anything, every Saturday. For the Bruma market, tel: (011) 622-9648.

Soweto: fascinating tours in South Africa's most famous township. For information call the Johannesburg Tourism Association, *see page 10*.

EVENTS AND FESTIVALS

South African PGA Golf Tournament: International and Southern African golfing greats meet in **Jan** to fight it out for this prestigious title.

Rand Show: in **Apr** the National Exhibition Centre (southwest of Johannesburg) hosts the biggest consumer show in Africa, featuring local and international products.

Johannesburg Pops Festival: in **Apr** traditional and contemporary musicians, choirs and soloists get together for the most vibrant 3-day outdoor concert in Southern Africa.

International Eisteddfod of South Africa: during **Sep/Oct** in the city of **Roodepoort** musicians and dancers from around the world compete for honours in this cultural event.

Gay and Lesbian Pride: original, largest local gay and lesbian celebration, **Sep**.

Encounters: South Africa's only film festival devoted exclusively to documentaries; **Jul-Aug**, features screenings, panel discussions and workshops.

ACCOMMODATION

Sandton Sun and Tower, Sandton City, tel: (011) 780-5000, fax: 780-5002; luxurious accommodation.

Rosebank Hotel, tel: (011) 447-2700, fax: 447-3276; well located; excellent reputation.

The Grace, Rosebank, tel: (011) 280-7200, fax: 280-7474; small five-star hotel.

Caesar's Palace, Kempton Park, tel/fax: (011) 928-1001; luxurious, upmarket casino complex.

Gold Reef Protea Hotel, tel: (011) 248-5700, fax: (011) 248-5791; Victorian charm, located right in the theme park.

City Lodge Morningside, tel: (011) 884-9500, fax: 884-9440; just 30 min from the airport in lovely Sandton.

Holiday Inn Garden Court Milpark, Auckland Park, tel: (011) 726-5100, fax: 726-8615; 6km (4 miles) from the city centre.

Karos Johannesburger, tel: (011) 725-3753, fax: 725-6309; located in the heart of town.

Airport Formule 1, tel: (011) 392-1453, fax: 974-3845; budget; close to the International Airport.

City Lodge Airport, tel: (011) 392-1750, fax: 392-2644; 5 min from airport.

B&B Association (central booking office), tel: (011) 783-3033, fax: 884-4442.

Lolo's Guesthouse, tel: (011) 988-4102, fax: (011) 988-4102; award-winning establishment where Mrs Mabitsela, a retired teacher, shares her wealth of first-hand knowledge of the turbulence in Soweto in the 70s with her guests.

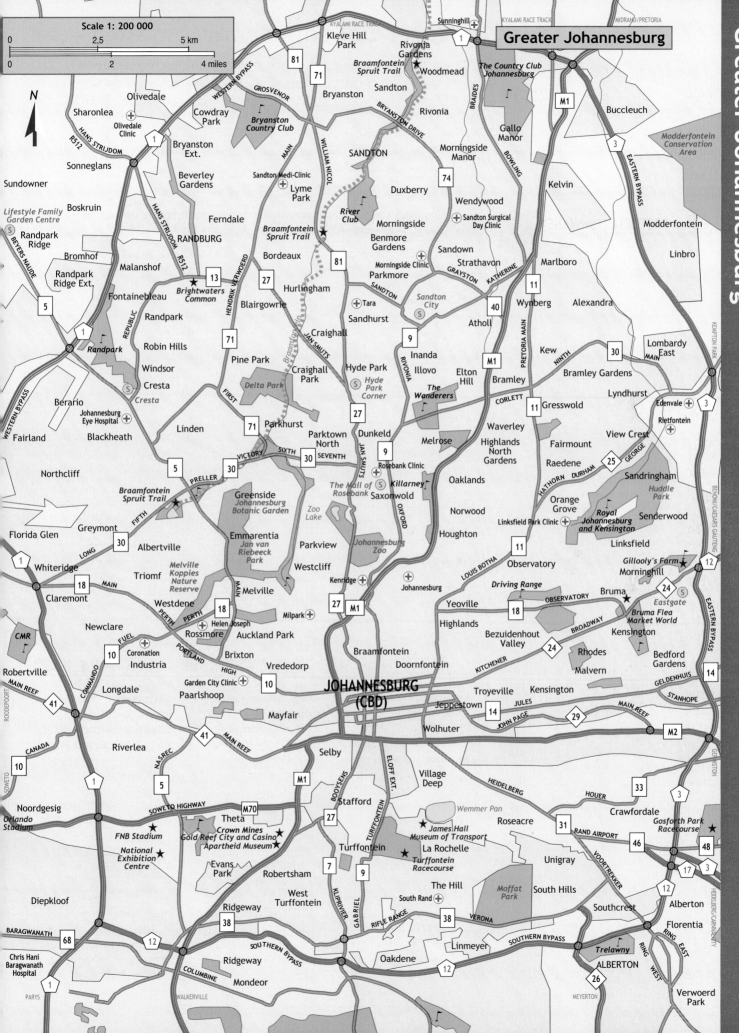

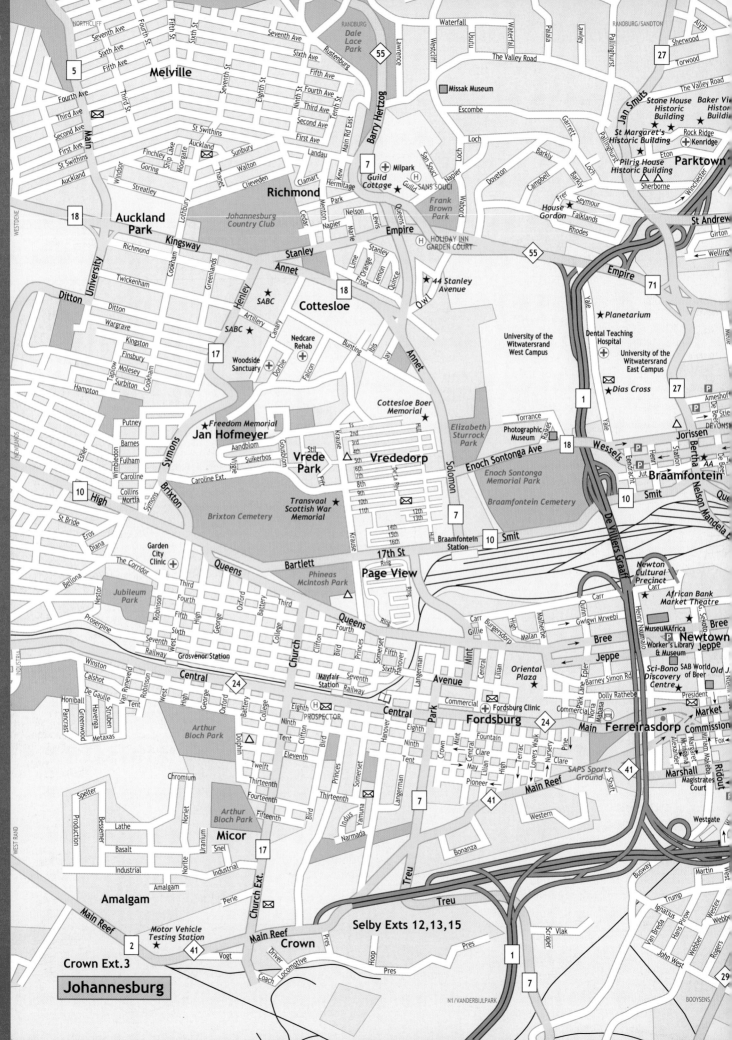

Johannesburg

Crown Ext. 3

Pretoria (Tshwane)

Handsome Pretoria is noted for its stately, historic homes, the impressive Union Buildings (home to major departments of the national government), its parks and gardens with their splendid wealth of flora, and for its tall jacaranda trees that transform the streets into a blaze of lilac each October/November, earning Pretoria its nickname, 'Jacaranda City'. The city is the administrative capital of the country, as well as a centre of research and learning. Within its limits lie the Pretoria University; gigantic Unisa, among the world's largest distance-learning institutions; and Onderstepoort, an internationally renowned veterinary research institute.

Above: *Summertime in Pretoria is heralded by a glory of lilac blossoms as the many jacaranda trees begin to flower, covering city streets and walks with a fragrant, pastel-coloured carpet.*

MAIN ATTRACTIONS

Union Buildings:
magnificent edifice designed by Sir Herbert Baker overlooking the city from Meintjieskop. To view the lovely gardens, tel: (012) 300-5200.

Church Square:
historic town square framed by beautiful old buildings such as the old Raadsaal (parliament), Palace of Justice and SA Reserve Bank.

Voortrekker Monument:
construction on Monument Hill, 6km (4 miles) from the city, commemorating the Great Trek of the 1830 pioneers.

National Zoological Gardens:
one of the world's largest, over 3500 exotic and indigenous species, tel: (012) 328-3265, fax: 323-4540.

Transvaal Museum of Natural History:
extensive displays, including the impressive 'Life's Genesis' and the Austin Roberts Bird Hall, tel: (012) 322-7632, fax: 322-7939.

State Theatre:
on completion in 1981, this cultural complex, comprising five theatres and a public square, was the largest of its kind in the southern hemisphere, tel: (012) 392-4000, fax: 322-3913.

ACCOMMODATION

Centurion Lake Hotel, 1001 Lenchen Avenue North, Centurion, tel: (012) 663-1825, fax: 643-3636.
Holiday Inn Pretoria, cnr Beatrix and Church streets, Arcadia, tel: (012) 341-1571, fax: 440-7534; centrally located.
Arcadia Hotel, tel: (012) 326-9311, fax: 326-1067; beautifully situated right at the foot of the impressive Union Buildings.

Bentley's Country Lodge, cnr Main Street and Brits Road, Akasia, tel: (012) 542-1751, fax: 542-3487.
The Farm Inn, Lynnwood Road, The Willows, tel: (012) 809-0266, fax: 809-0146; beautiful game farm close to the city, next to Silverlakes Golf Club; recently opened 4x4 track.
Victoria Hotel, cnr Scheiding and Paul Kruger streets, tel: (012) 323-6054, fax: 324-2426.

USEFUL CONTACTS

Pretoria Tourist Information Centre, Church Square, tel: (012) 337-4430, fax: 358-1485.
International Embassies, all on dialling code (012):
• Australia, tel: 342-3740
• France, tel: 425-1600, fax: 425-1609
• Germany, tel: 427-8900, fax: 343-9401
• Italy, tel: 423-0000, fax: 430-5547
• Netherlands, tel: 425-4500,
• Spain, tel: 344-3877, fax: 343-4891
• UK, tel: 421-7500, fax: 483-1302
• USA, tel: 431-4000, fax: 342-2244.

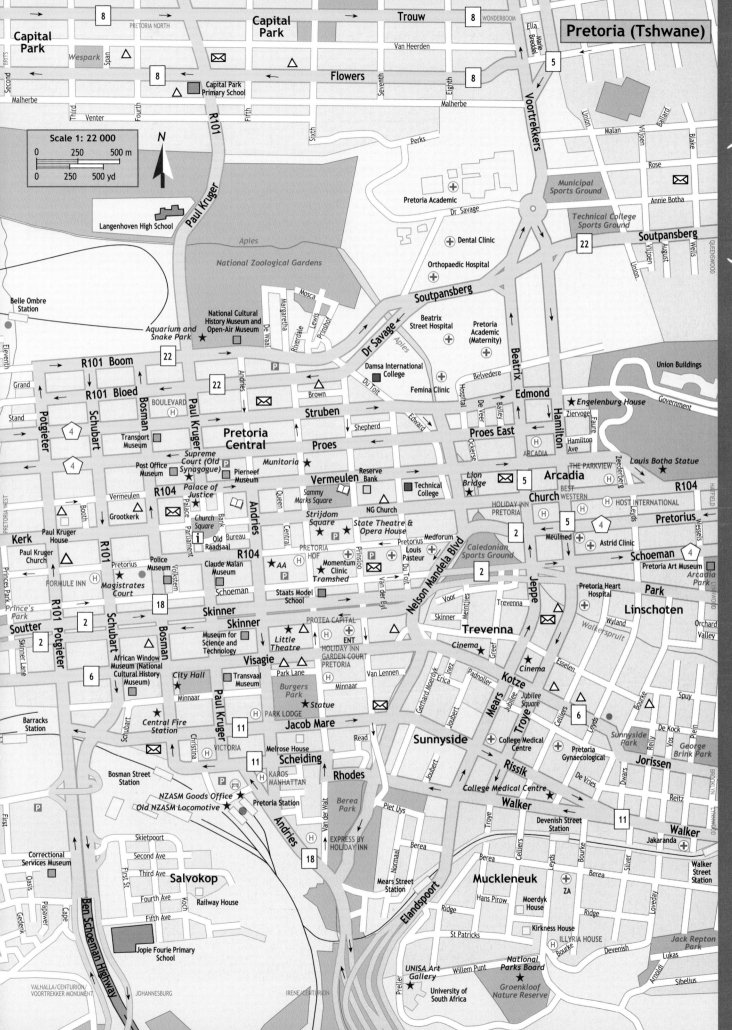

Pilanesberg and Sun City

*T*he dramatic Lost City and Sun City leisure resort, one of South Africa's most glittering tourist venues featuring casinos, bars, restaurants, hotels, theatres, nightclubs and shops, is set among the lush vegetation of beautifully landscaped grounds, in what before was little more than desert territory. Apart from the 31,500m^2 (339,063ft^2) Valley of the Waves, a man-made water park with soft sand beaches, waterslides, cascades and 1.8m-high (5.9ft) waves, the complex also offers an Arizona Desert-style golf course where crocodiles lie in wait at the 13th hole, and another at the Gary Player Country Club, venue of the annual Million Dollar Golf Challenge. Musicians such as Queen and Elton John have also performed at the Sun City Super Bowl, a large auditorium which seats 6200. Pilanesberg Game Reserve north of Sun City has some 10,000 head of wildlife including the Big Five — buffalo, rhino (black and white), elephant, lion and leopard — and over 300 bird species. This game-rich habitat lies within four concentric mountain rings, the relics of an ancient volcano. In the centre of the bowl is Mankwe Dam, a favourite hippo haunt. The park is traversed by a network of game-viewing roads; guided walks and drives are conducted and hot-air balloon trips can be organized. This wonderful park is the result of 'Operation Genesis', a successful game-stocking venture. A visit to the aviary at Manyane Gate should not be missed.

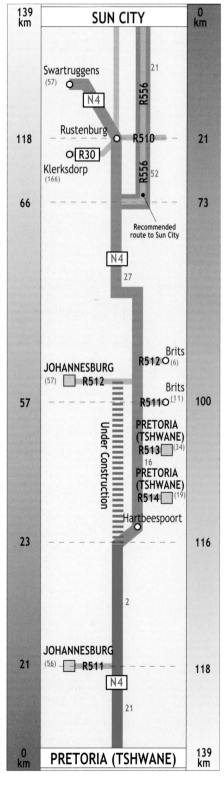

ACCOMMODATION

Sun City complex,
tel: (014) 557-1000, fax: 557-4210.
The Cascades, tel: (014) 557-5420.
Palace of the Lost City, the ultimate in luxurious extravagance.
Sun City Cabanas, mainly family-oriented and affordable.
Sun City Main Hotel, superb five-star comfort surrounded by subtropical gardens.

Pilanesberg National Park,
tel: (014) 555-5351, fax: 555-5525.
Bakubung Game Lodge,
tel: (014) 552-6000, fax: 552-6300; thatched rooms around a hippo pool in a private game reserve.
Kwa Maritane Lodge,
tel: (014) 552-5100, fax: 552-5333; luxurious accommodation in the African bush.

USEFUL CONTACTS

Pilanesberg Game Reserve,
tel: (014) 555-5351; for the real bush experience.

Below: *Fabled to be the royal residence of an ancient king, the Palace of the Lost City rises dramatically out of the surrounding African bush, like the legendary temple of a mysterious civilization.*

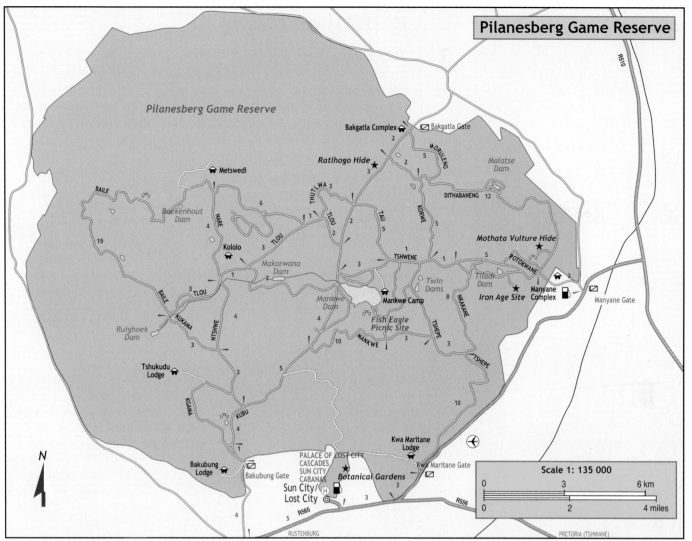

Pilanesberg Game Reserve

Pilanesberg Game Reserve

Bakgatla Complex
Bakgatla Gate
Ratlhogo Hide ★
Metswedi
MORULENG
Malatse Dam
BAILE
DITHABANENG 12
Boekenhout Dam
THUTLWA
TLOU
TAU
KORWE
Mothata Vulture Hide ★
NARE
TLOU
Kololo
TSHWENE
POTOKWANE
Makorwana Dam
Twin Dams
Titodi Dam
Manyane Complex
BAILE
TLOU
Iron Age Site ★
Manyane Gate
KUKAMA
NTSHWE
Mankwe Dam
Mankwe Camp
NKAKANE
Ruighoek Dam
Fish Eagle Picnic Site
TSHEPE
Tshukudu Lodge
MANKWE
TSHEPE
KGAMA
KUBU
Kwa Maritane Lodge
Bakubung Lodge
PALACE OF LOST CITY
CASCADES
SUN CITY
CABANAS
Kwa Maritane Gate
Bakubung Gate
Botanical Gardens
Sun City/ Lost City
R565
R556
RUSTENBURG
PRETORIA (TSHWANE)
R510

Scale 1: 135 000
0   3   6 km
0   2   4 miles

N

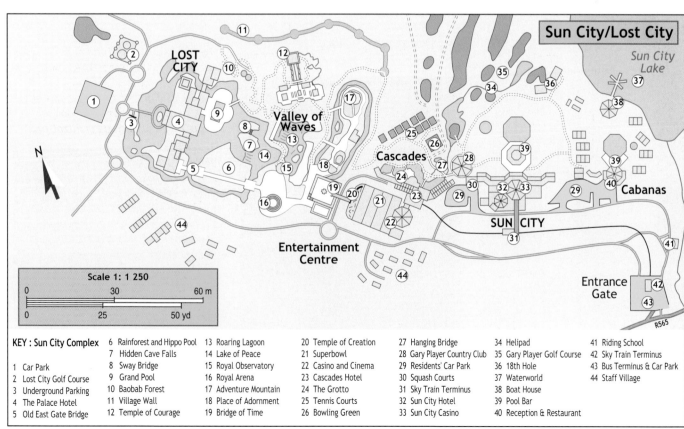

Sun City/Lost City

LOST CITY
11
2
10
12
1
3
9
8
17
Valley of Waves
13
7
14
5
6
15
16
18
19
20
21
22
23
24
25
26
27
28
Cascades
Hanging Bridge
29
30
31
32
33
SUN CITY
29
39
35
34
36
Sun City Lake
37
38
39
40
Cabanas
41
42
43
44
44
Entertainment Centre
Entrance Gate
R565
N

Scale 1: 1 250
0   30   60 m
0   25   50 yd

KEY : Sun City Complex

1 Car Park
2 Lost City Golf Course
3 Underground Parking
4 The Palace Hotel
5 Old East Gate Bridge
6 Rainforest and Hippo Pool
7 Hidden Cave Falls
8 Sway Bridge
9 Grand Pool
10 Baobab Forest
11 Village Wall
12 Temple of Courage
13 Roaring Lagoon
14 Lake of Peace
15 Royal Observatory
16 Royal Arena
17 Adventure Mountain
18 Place of Adornment
19 Bridge of Time
20 Temple of Creation
21 Superbowl
22 Casino and Cinema
23 Cascades Hotel
24 The Grotto
25 Tennis Courts
26 Bowling Green
27 Hanging Bridge
28 Gary Player Country Club
29 Residents' Car Park
30 Squash Courts
31 Sky Train Terminus
32 Sun City Hotel
33 Sun City Casino
34 Helipad
35 Gary Player Golf Course
36 18th Hole
37 Waterworld
38 Boat House
39 Pool Bar
40 Reception & Restaurant
41 Riding School
42 Sky Train Terminus
43 Bus Terminus & Car Park
44 Staff Village

Kruger National Park

*S*outh Africa's premier wildlife sanctuary covers more than 20,000 km² (7720 sq miles) — an area about the size of Wales and larger than the state of Israel. Because this vast, wild expanse encompasses many different habitats, it is a haven for more varieties of wildlife than any other conservation area in Africa. Among the estimated 140 mammal species occurring here are the Big Five: lion (approximately 1500), elephant (about 8000), leopard (around 1000), buffalo (25,000), and rhino, both black and white. Other large wildlife populations include zebra, wildebeest, giraffe, hippo and crocodile, as well as some 500 bird species. If you are lucky, you may even spot a pack of the increasingly rare wild dogs.

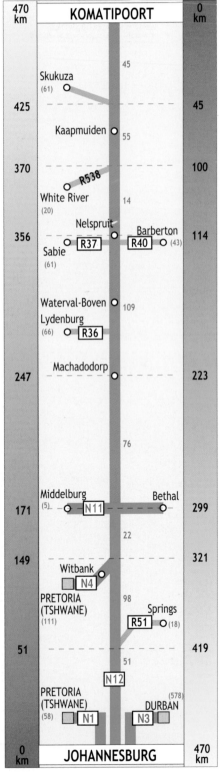

470 km	KOMATIPOORT	0 km
	Skukuza (61)	
	45	
425		45
	Kaapmuiden 55	
370		100
	R538	
	White River (20) 14	
	Nelspruit	
356	R37 R40 (43) Barberton	114
	Sabie (61)	
	Waterval-Boven 109	
	Lydenburg (66) R36	
	Machadodorp	
247		223
	76	
	Middelburg (5) N11 Bethal	
171		299
	22	
149		321
	Witbank N4	
	PRETORIA (TSHWANE) (111) 98 Springs	
	R51 (18)	
51		419
	51	
	N12	
	PRETORIA (TSHWANE) (58) N1 DURBAN (578) N3	
0 km	JOHANNESBURG	470 km

TRAVEL TIPS

An extensive network, consisting of about 880km (550 miles) of tarred surface and 1700km (1060 miles) of gravel road, traverses the park, providing effective access to all areas of the Kruger. Should you experience any car trouble, vehicle breakdown services are available at Skukuza and Letaba camps. A few general safety guidelines have to be observed by all visitors:

- Malaria treatment should be started prior to entering this area (consult your physician), and use insect repellent.
- Stay on the designated roads or tracks.
- Keep to the speed limit.
- Do not leave your vehicle.
- Don't injure, feed or disturb wildlife.
- Littering is an offence.
- Be sure to arrive at your rest camp by the stipulated time before sunset.

MAIN ATTRACTIONS

The Big Five can be viewed in their natural environment. To view, try the **Pafuri area** in the far north. **Water holes** attract a steady parade of wildlife. Overnight visitors have a choice of 20 or so comfortable, tree-shaded **rest camps**, of which **Skukuza** is the largest, boasting all the amenities of a small town. **Olifants Camp**, perched on high cliffs, offers splendid vistas. Smaller and more intimate are the **bush camps**. **Tshokwane** is among several attractive **picnic spots**; Nwanetsi, which overlooks the Sweni River, is an especially rewarding **look-out post**. A number of **wilderness trails** offer the ultimate bush experience. **Private game lodges** provide luxury, personal service and superb game-viewing. Popular spots include Sabi Sabi, Londolozi and Mala Mala. Check out the following website for a list of lodges in the area, www.places.co.za

Left: *Elephants should always be approached with caution. Warning signals, which include a raised trunk and flapping ears, should never be ignored. Elephants are voracious feeders which daily consume up to 272 Kg (600 lb) of grass, tender shoots and bark from trees. The elephant's sensitive trunk can even detect water underground. An adult elephant can drink up to 200 litres of water in a single session.*

ACCOMMODATION

Over 20 pleasant, clean and safe rest camps are located within the park. For reservations contact the **National Parks Board**, tel: (012) 428-9111, fax: 343-0905, website: www.sanparks.org

Kruger National Park

Camp Gate & Entry Gate Timetable

OPEN

	JAN	FEB	MAR	APR	MAY-JUL	AUG-SEPT	OCT	NOV-DEC
	4:30	5:30	5:30	6:00	6:00	6:00	5:30	4:30

CLOSE

	JAN	FEB	MAR	APR	MAY-AUG	SEPT	OCT	NOV-DEC
	18:30	18:30	18:00	18:00	17:30	18:00	18:00	18:30

ENTRY GATES OPEN: JAN 5:30 NOV-DEC 5:30

PARK REGULATIONS

Speed Limit: Tarred rds-50 kph; Gravel rds-40 kph
Only leave car at selected viewpoints
Stay on road and do not feed animals

CAMP REGULATIONS

There may be no noise between 21:30 & 06:00
No roller-skating, skateboarding & cycling
No trading or advertising is permitted
Speed limit within rest camp is 10 kph
No pets allowed & firearms must be declared

MAIN CAMP SITE — Overnight accommodation & facilities for day visitors.
BUSHVELD CAMP — Overnight accommodation & camping.
PRIVATE CAMP — No facilities for day visitors, no entry without booking.
TRAIL BASE CAMP — Walking trails, no day visitor facilities, no entry without booking.

Scale 1: 600 000

0   10   20 km

0   5   10 miles

Mpumalanga Drakensberg

*M*ountainous terrain, misty forests, bushveld and endless views are the compelling features of this escarpment region far to the east of Gauteng, across the great Highveld plateau. For sheer scenic beauty, few parts of the Southern African subcontinent can compare with the Great Escarpment, a spectacular wonderland of buttresses, sculpted peaks and deep ravines. The Olifants and Crocodile rivers and a score of their tributaries run through verdant valleys. One tributary, the Blyde River, over centuries carved a canyon that now ranks as one of Africa's great scenic splendours.

MAIN ATTRACTIONS

Blyde River Canyon: a majestic gorge whose sheer cliff faces plunge to the water far below.

Bourke's Luck Potholes: a fantasia of hollowed-out rocks.

Pilgrim's Rest: town born out of the 1870 gold rush, now a quaint, living museum.

Jock of the Bushveld: trail begins in Graskop for the heroic dog in the novel by Sir Percy FitzPatrick.

God's Window: for the most magnificent views of the area.

Mount Sheba: beautiful forest reserve high in the mountains.

Magoebaskloof: large tracts of thick indigenous forest.

Long Tom Pass: spectacular pass between Sabie and Lydenburg.

Echo Caves: archaeological evidence of earlier inhabitants.

The Trout Triangle: area around Waterval-Boven, Dullstroom and Lydenburg; popular with nature-lovers and the fly-fishing elite.

Swadini Reptile Park: with snakes, lizards and crocodiles. Interesting presentations and commentaries and, for those so inclined, the chance of handling a snake (under supervision).

TRAVEL TIPS

The region has an excellent network of roads. Travelling from Johannesburg to Nelspruit and the escarpment, take the R22 and then the N4 near Witbank; from Pretoria take the N4 direct. The R40 leads from Nelspruit north into the escarpment. Alternatively, follow the N1 national highway from Pretoria; turn right at Polokwane (Pietersburg) on the R71 for Tzaneen and the central region of the Kruger National Park (around Phalaborwa). If you intend travelling into the far northern region of the park, take the R524 at Louis Trichardt. Please note: this is a **malaria** area so ensure that the necessary precautions are taken before travelling into this area; for more information on the hazards, consult your physician.

ACCOMMODATION

Mount Sheba Hotel, west of Pilgrim's Rest, tel: (013) 768-1241, fax: 768-1248; luxury hotel.

Sabi River Sun, close to Paul Kruger Gate, tel: (013) 737-7311, fax: 737-7314; 18-hole golf course.

Pine Lake Sun, White River, tel: (013) 750-0709, fax: 751-3873; on the edge of a lake; golf course.

Royal Hotel, Pilgrim's Rest, tel: (013) 768-1100, fax: 768-1188; stay in a national monument.

Critchley Hackle, Dullstroom, tel: (013) 254-0149, fax: 254-0262.

Malapo Country Lodge, Lydenburg, tel: (013) 235-1056, fax: (013) 235-2398; with ASTRO Boma (open-air Observatory) where African star lore comes alive.

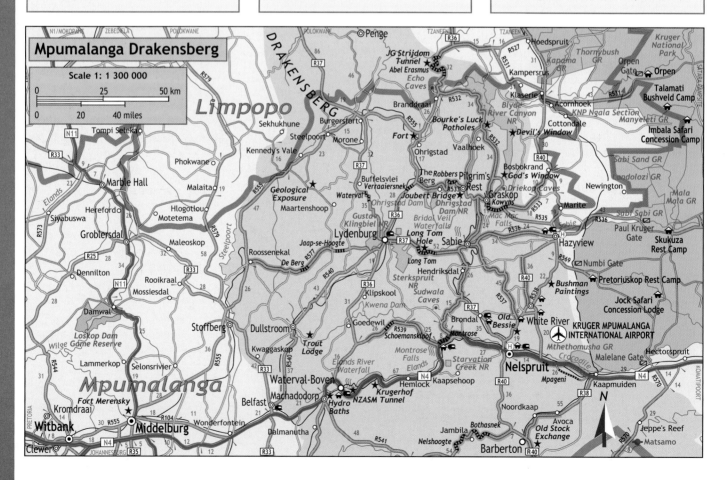

Nelspruit

Largest town in, and capital of, Mpumalanga is Nelspruit, set on the Crocodile River in the warm, undulating grasslands below the escarpment and centre of a beautiful and immensely fertile area. It's an attractive little city of wide streets lined with poinciana trees that, during the summer months, are ablaze with deep red blossoms. Nelspruit is the last major town on the southern route to the Kruger National Park; among its attractions are excellent hotels and restaurants, modern shopping centres and speciality outlets that cater well for the tourist.

MAIN ATTRACTIONS

Lowveld Botanic Gardens: on the Crocodile River, supporting over 500 species of indigenous flora.

Lowveld Herbarium: adjacent to the Gardens; of interest to the botanist as well as the layperson.

Sudwala Caves: dramatic cave formations and an interesting dinosaur park, about 40km (25 miles) northwest of Nelspruit.

Riverside Trail: self-guided 4km (2.5-mile) hike along the Crocodile River, with some lovely waterfalls.

Farm stalls: roadside stalls around the town sell fresh fruit and curios.

Barberton Museum Complex: opened in 1994; gives a comprehensive picture of the history, geology, archaeology and ethnology of the region.

ACCOMMODATION

Cybele Forest Lodge, R40, White River, tel: (013) 764-1823, fax: 764-9510; exclusive retreat surrounded by nature.

Hotel The Winkler, tel: (013) 751-5068, fax: 751-5044; in the beautiful White River area.

Premier Lodge, Graniet Street, Nelspruit, tel: (013) 741-4222.

The Rest Country Lodge, tel: (013) 744-9991, fax: (013) 744-9472; luxury suites near Nelspruit.

Lowveld Lodge, Kastings Street, White River, tel: (013) 750-0206.

USEFUL CONTACTS

Rob Ferreira Hospital, tel: (013) 741-3031.

WATERFALL ROUTE

There are some beautiful waterfalls in the Sabie/Graskop area about 50km (31 miles) north of Nelspruit. The falls are worth a visit and are easily accessible on a good road network. Among the best falls to view are:

Bridal Veil: a delicate spray of water surrounded by a forest echoing with the calls of many birds; 7km (4.2 miles) north of Sabie.

Mac Mac: twin cascades plunge 56m (185ft) into a deep, green ravine.

Lone Creek: hidden some 68m (222ft) in a beautiful, misty forest.

Horseshoe: a national monument.

Berlin: plunges about 48m (158ft) into a deep pool.

Lisbon: picturesque double waterfall in a setting of special beauty.

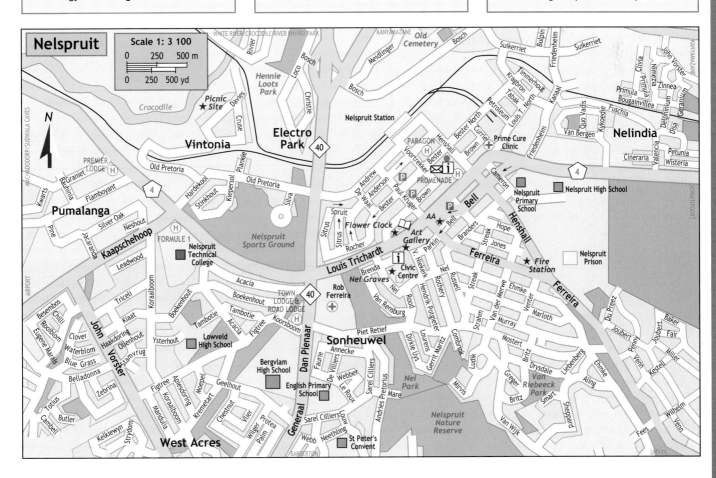

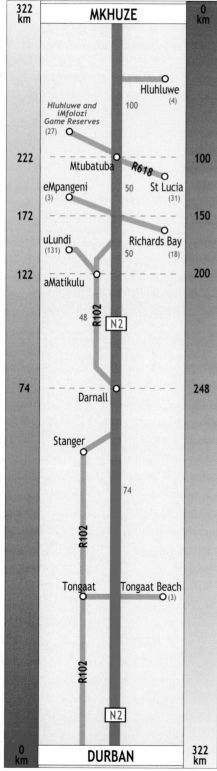

KwaZulu-Natal North Coast

*R*emarkable for its rich fauna and flora, northern KwaZulu-Natal boasts some of South Africa's finest game reserves (among them the Hluhluwe and iMfolozi Game Reserves, oldest of South Africa's many wildlife sanctuaries) and one of the world's great wetland and marine conservation areas, now a World Heritage Site, the Greater St Lucia Wetland Park. Just north of Durban, along the Dolphin Coast that stretches for 90km (55 miles) up to the Tugela River mouth, lies the upmarket resort town of uMhlanga Rocks. Beyond lies the area historically known as Zululand, whose largest centre and industrial hub is Richards Bay, notable for its busy deep-water harbour. The beaches, fringed by tropical vegetation, attract sunbathers, anglers, divers and boating enthusiasts.

MAIN ATTRACTIONS

Beaches: some excellent beaches north of Durban include uMhlanga Rocks, Tongaat, Ballito, Shaka's Rock, Salt Rock, Shelly Beach, North Beach (Margate) and uVongo.

Natal Sharks Board: in uMhlanga; enjoy an informative audiovisual presentation.

Lake Sibaya: South Africa's largest natural freshwater lake.

The Elephant Coast: recently declared a World Heritage Site and among the world's most ecologically diverse sanctuaries. Contact St Lucia Publicity Association, tel: (035) 590-1075/1247.

Maputaland Reserves: host some of the greatest concentrations of wildlife in South Africa.

The **Hluhluwe and iMfolozi Game Reserves:** famed for their rhino conservation programme and offering a haven for the Big Five, tel: (035) 562-0848 (Hilltop Camp), tel: (035) 562-0133 (Mpila Camp).

Phinda Resource Reserve: one of the best ecotourism destinations in South Africa, tel: (035) 562-0271, fax: 562-0399.

Sodwana Bay: marine wonderland, the best diving venue in South Africa, tel: (035) 571-0051/2/3.

Shakaland: model of a traditional Zulu village in the Nkwaleni Valley; includes culinary specialities, tribal dancing and traditional healers, tel: (035) 460-0912.

TRAVEL TIPS

The N2 runs parallel to, but mostly out of sight of, the coast to the eMpangeni-Richards Bay area (north of Durban), and then sweeps inland to the Swaziland border. Major roads in Zululand are tarred; most of the minor ones (including those in the game reserves) are gravel and generally in a satisfactory condition.

USEFUL CONTACTS

Dolphin Coast Tourism, tel: (032) 946-1997.

Isle of Capri, tel: (031) 337-7751, fax: (031) 305-3099; deep-sea cruises and fishing trips.

Natal Sharks Board, tel: (031) 566-0400.

Below: *The golden sands of St Lucia.*

KwaZulu-Natal North Coast

CANDOVER/SWAZILAND

PONGOLA

ROOI RAND

LEBOMBO MOUNTAIN

MBAZWANA

Mkhuze

Mantuma
Nhlonhlela

Ghost Mtn
529m

▲ Mkhuzi Game Reserve
Mkhuze Game Reserve Rest Camps

Mosi Swamp

Yengweni Pan

Sodwana Bay NP

Uquandu
Mbaswana

Lake Bhangazi North

Sihlepu

Kwa Mnyaise

UDANGASELE RIDGE

Nsumu Pan

Sodwana Bay State Forest

R66

Ngome

Toggekry

Dlomodlomo

DLOMODLOMO

UMSWETI RANGE

Ngamudi 657 m

Bongonoma

Bayala

Phinda Resource Reserve

Bhumbeni Game Reserve

Panata Game Reserve

Ekuseni

Umzene Game Ranch

Ochre Hill 129m

The Greater St Lucia Wetland Park (World Heritage Site)

Mkhuze Swamp

Nongoma

R618

Mduna

Mhlosinga

AMAHLUMBE RANGE

Makowe

Ngweni

False Bay Park

Tewate Wilderness Area

St Mary's Hill

Leven Point 146m

Kleinbegin Guest House

False Bay

Bird Island

Lake St Lucia

Lane Island

St Lucia Marine Reserve

Hluhluwe Game Reserve

Ubizane Beehives

Hluhluwe

Dugandlovu

Zulu Nyala Game Lodge

Hilltop Camp/Mtwazi Lodge

Insimane 657 m

Zululand Tree Lodge
iSinkiwe Backpackers Lodge

Bushlands Game Lodge

Ncemane

Uncle Jim's Cottage

Malalá Lodge

Bushlands

Lake Bhangazi South

▲ Pembeni

Muntulu Bush Lodge

Hlabisa

Thiyeni Waterhole

Hluhluwe Dam

Mfekayi

Fanie's Island

Banghazi

Cape Vidal

Munyawaneni Bush Lodge

Ntondweni
382 m

Western Shores

Eastern Shores

Mona

Mahlabatini

Sontuli

Centenary Game Capture Centre

Nagana

Nyalazi River

Charter's Creek

Mission Rocks

Mpande's Kraal

Cetshwayo's Kraal

uLundi

Nodwengu

uLundi

Gqoyeni

Nselweni

Masinda

Mpila

Somkele

Fernwood

Narrows

iMfolozi Game Reserve

Shaka's Hunting Pits

Dukuduku

Crocodile Centre

St Lucia

Ndini

Mtjonjaneni

White Mfolozi

Mtubatuba

River View

St Lucia Bay

Mfolozi Estuary

Mapelane

Mfolozi Swamp

Lake Eteza NR

Cape St Lucia Lighthouse

Sangoyana

KwaZulu-Natal

Monzi

Lakeview

Umfolozi

Lake Eteza NR

Teza

Red Hill 175 m

Cape St Lucia

Melmoth

Upper Nseleni

Ntambanana

Kwa Magwaza

Tatafalaza

R34

Ndundulu

Heatonville

Mposa

Nselemi

KwaMbonambi

Nhlabane Lake (Lake Mzingazi)

INDIAN OCEAN

Ekutuleni

Nkwalini

Nsimbakazi

R34

eNseleni NR

Insese Lake

Mhlatuzi

Site of Shaka's Kraal

eMpangeni

Sta.

Hibberds

Imfule

Mpofu 643 m

Coward's Bush Monument

Ngwelezana

Richards Bay

Mhlatuzi Lagoon

eShowe North

R66

Felixton

Esikhawini

Richards Bay Nature Reserve

Uqupa Lake

aMatikulu

Mandini

Tugela

Ultimatum Tree

Tugela Mouth

Fort Pearson

eShowe

Fort KwaMondi

Mzingwenya

Darnall

Zinkwazi Beach

Fort Nongayi

Mtunzini

Port Durnford

Port Durnford Lighthouse

Stanger

Shaka's Memorial

Blackburn

uMlazi Nature Reserve

Raffia Palms

Groutville

Blythdale Beach

Gingindlovu

Nyezane

Hudley

Shakaskraal

Sheffield Beach

Salt Rock

Shaka's Rock

Compensation Beach

aMatikulu

Nyoni

Tongaat

Ballito

Tongaat Beach

iSithebe

Ndwedwe

INDIAN OCEAN

Sundumbili

Mandini

Verulam

iNanda

La Mercy

uMdloti

Tugela

Newark

Krantzkloof NR

uMhlanga

Stanger

Ultimatum Tree
Fort Pearson

KwaMashu

Clermont

Pinetown

Westville

Queensburgh

The Bluff

DURBAN

uMlazi

Dick King's House

SEE INSET

Scale 1: 640 000

0   20   40 km

0   10   20 miles

N

KwaZulu-Natal South Coast

*T*he seaboard running south from Durban to the Eastern Cape border, or Mtamvuna River, is known as the South Coast. It is one of the southern hemisphere's most entrancing holiday regions, a subtropical wonderland of wide, unspoilt beaches lapped by the warm blue waters of the Indian Ocean, of a lushly green hinterland, and of a score and more sunlit towns, villages and hamlets, each with its special personality and attractions. Part of the long shoreline, that which runs from Hibberdene to Port Edward, is also referred to as the Hibiscus Coast.

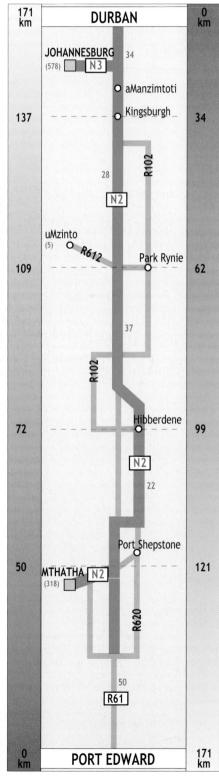

MAIN ATTRACTIONS

South Coast
Kingsburgh: five seaside resorts popular for their white sands and shark-protected bathing.
uMkomaas: a championship golf course and floodlit tidal pool.
Scottburgh: a charming beach, and fascinating Crocworld nearby.
Vernon Crookes Nature Reserve: lush sanctuary for various antelope.

Hibiscus Coast
Hibberdene: lagoon, woodland-fringed beaches, amusement park.
uMzumbe: excellent family hotel; rock and surf angling.
Banana Beach: safe bathing and very good surfing.
Bendigo: four seaside resorts geared towards holiday-makers.

uMtentweni: for a quiet getaway.
Port Shepstone: at the mouth of the Mzimkulu River; offers excellent bowling greens and one of South Africa's best golf courses.
Oribi Gorge Nature Reserve: some 20km (14 miles) inland from Port Shepstone — a striking canyon carved through layers of sandstone by the Mzimkulwana River.
uVongo: lively little resort in an idyllic tropical setting.
Margate: very popular seaside town, but it can get crowded.
Ramsgate: magnificent lagoon and a long beach.
Port Edward: charming town in the former Transkei, with a pleasant beach; close to the Wild Coast Sun.

Above: *Scottburgh is a popular holiday resort on the South Coast. The lovely beach offers safe bathing, as well as some fine angling spots.*

USEFUL CONTACTS

Hospital GJ Crookes, Scottburgh, tel: (039) 978-7000.
Hibiscus Coast Tourism, Margate, tel: (039) 312-2322, fax: 317-4650.
Scottburgh Tourism, tel: (039) 976-1364, fax: 978-3114.

TRAVEL TIPS

Towns and resorts are linked to Durban by the N2 as far as Port Shepstone, while the R61 leads to Port Edward. Both roads are in good condition, though inland roads can be a little rough and caution is advised.

KwaZulu-Natal South Coast

Scale 1: 640 000

0   20   40 km

0   10   20 miles

N

LESOTHO
PIETERMARITZBURG
KwaZulu-Natal
Eastern Cape
DURBAN
Eastern Cape
● Port Edward

Durban and Pietermaritzburg

*T*he city of Durban is South Africa's third largest metropolis, foremost seaport (the harbour is ranked ninth in the world in terms of size and traffic) and among the country's most popular holiday destinations. Durban and it's subtropical surrounds offer many varied attractions: the beachfront, known as the Golden Mile, with its superb beaches (protected by anti-shark nets) for sunbathing, swimming and surfing; hotels, nightspots, restaurants, glittering shopping malls, pleasant parks and, in parts, an appealingly exotic atmosphere conferred by the city's large Indian community.

ACCOMMODATION

Royal Hotel, 267 Smith Street, tel: (031) 333-6000, fax: 333-6002; one of the best; luxury.
Holiday Inn Garden Court (South Beach), tel: (031) 337-2231, fax: 337-4640; stylish and comfortable.
Holiday Inn Garden Court (Marine Parade), tel: (031) 337-3341, fax: 337-5929.
Balmoral Hotel, 125 Marine Parade, tel: (031) 368-5940, fax: 368-5955; situated right across the road from the beach.
Four Seasons, Gillespie Street, tel: (031) 337-3381, fax: 337-3380; rooms offering sea views.
Protea Hotel Imperial, 224 Loop Street, Pietermaritzburg, tel: (033) 342-6551, fax: 342-9796; central; colonial atmosphere.
Crossways Country Inn, Old Howick Road, just north of Pietermaritzburg, tel: (033) 343-3267, fax: 343-3273; English pub atmosphere.
Rawdon's, Old Main Road, Nottingham Road, tel: (033) 266-6044, fax: 266-6048; exquisite English country-style homestead.

MAIN ATTRACTIONS

Golden Mile: fabulous holiday playground stretching along the sandy Indian Ocean shoreline.
uShaka Marine World: on the Golden Mile, popular aquarium-dolphinarium.
Fitzsimon's Snake Park: home to many snake species, as well as crocodiles, tel: 073 156 9606.
Victoria Street Indian Market: colourful and exotic place of bargain and barter.
uMgeni River Bird Park: rated third best of the world's bird parks, tel: (031) 579-4600.
Gandhi Settlement: visit the renovated farm where Gandhi once resided; situated in iNanda, tel: (031) 309-1951.
The Wheel: very lively and glitzy shopping complex, with restaurants and live entertainment.
Port Natal Maritime Museum: on the Victoria Embankment; interesting exhibits, tel: (031) 311-2230, fax: (031) 311-2230.
Pietermaritzburg: quaint colonial-style town; fine architecture; interesting museums. Home to two internationally renowned sports events, the Dusi Canoe Marathon and the Comrades Marathon.

EVENTS AND FESTIVALS

Howick: Midmar Mile swim marathon, held in **January**, sometimes **February**.
Comrades Marathon: famous marathon in **June** (Durban to Pietermaritzburg the one year, vice versa the following one).
July Handicap: prestigious horse-racing event in **July**.
Mr Price Pro: world-renowned annual surfing contest held in the Bay of Plenty in **July**.

USEFUL CONTACTS

Addington Hospital, tel: (031) 327-2000, fax: 327-2387.
Durban Africa, Tourist Junction Building, tel: (031) 304-4934, fax: 304-3868.
uShaka Marine World, 1 Bell Street, Durban, tel: (031) 328-8000, fax: 328-8090, website: www.ushakamarineworld.co.za
Pietermaritzburg Tourism, tel: (033) 345-1348, fax: 394-3535.

Right: *The Paddling Pools form part of Durban's sparkling Golden Mile. Other attractions on offer here include colourful markets, numerous restaurants, scenic walkways and fountains.*

TRAVEL TIPS

Durban's international airport is 15 minutes from the city centre. It is linked to all other major South African centres by a network of national roads. The N2 leads south and then west along the coast, through Port Elizabeth to Cape Town. The N3 takes the traveller northwest through Pietermaritzburg and Harrismith to Johannesburg.

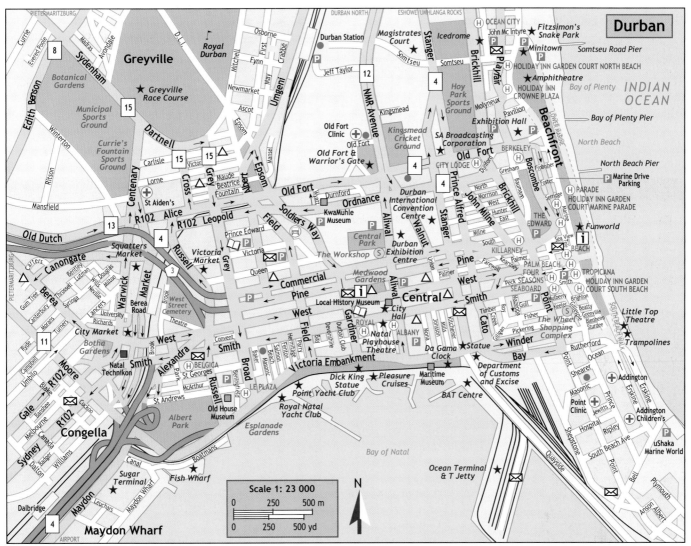

Durban

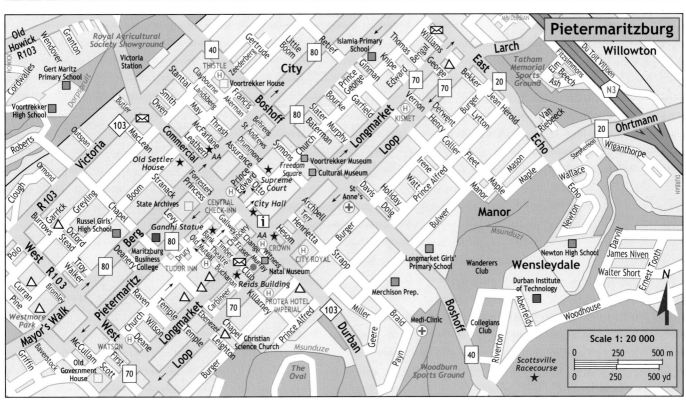

Pietermaritzburg

KwaZulu-Natal Drakensberg

*S*outh Africa's highest mountain range, the Drakensberg is a massive and strikingly beautiful rampart of deep gorges, pinnacles and saw-edged ridges, caves, overhangs and balancing rocks. In the winter months its upper levels lie deep in snow, but clustered among the foothills far below, in undulating grassland, is a score of resort hotels established and run for the most part for family holiday-makers. People come for the fresh, clean mountain air; for the walks, climbs and drives; for the gentler sports (trout fishing, golf, bowls and horseback riding); and for casual relaxation in the most exquisite surrounds.

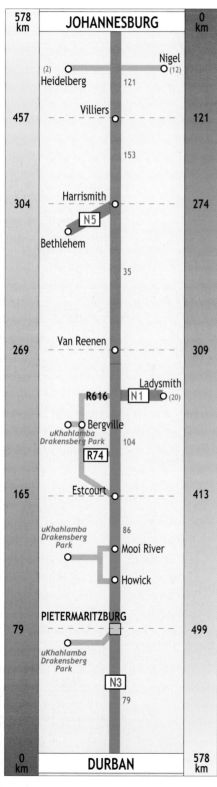

ACCOMMODATION

Cathedral Peak Hotel, Winterton, tel: (036) 488-1888, fax: 488-1889; set amid spectacular peaks.
Drakensberg Sun Hotel, in the central Drakensberg region, tel: (036) 468-1000, fax: 468-1224; wonderful views.
Little Switzerland Hotel, between Bergville and Harrismith, tel: (036) 438-6220, fax: 438-6222; view of the spectacular Amphitheatre.

Sani Pass Hotel, Himeville, tel: (033) 702-1320, fax: 702-0220; 800ha (1977 acres) situated at the foot of Sani Pass.
Champagne Castle, tel: (036) 468-1063, fax: 468-1306; guided walks; golf course.
Orion Mont-Aux-Sources, tel: (036) 438-6230, fax: 438-6201; 7km (4.3 miles) from the Royal Natal National Park.

MAIN ATTRACTIONS

Royal Natal National Park: an extensive and beautiful floral and wildlife sanctuary. Excursions to the Mont-Aux-Sources plateau and the spectacular Tugela Falls, the country's highest waterfall.
Champagne Castle: a magnificent peak and one of the Drakensberg's easier climbs.
Giant's Castle Game Reserve: in the central Drakensberg, a scenic wonderland famous for its Bushman rock art and raptor conservation programmes.
Ndedema Gorge: 'place of rolling thunder'; a magnificent gorge renowned for its rock art.
Himeville Nature Reserve: in the southern Drakensberg; a paradise for trout fishermen.
The Midlands Meander: a scenic route takes travellers through Meander outlets and picturesque villages. See art and craft studios, herb and flower farms, country pubs, breweries, and much more!

USEFUL CONTACTS

Drakensberg Tourism, tel/fax: (036) 448-1557.
Central Drakensberg Information, tel: (036) 488-1207, fax: 488-1846.
Mountain Club of SA, tel: (021) 465-3412.
Drakensberg Boys Choir School, tel: (036) 468-1012, except during school holidays.
Midlands Meander Tourism, for information tel: (033) 330-8195; website: www.midlandsmeander.org.za

Right: *The impressive Giant's Castle, formed by vast lava outpourings of the Drakensberg Basalt Formation (to a thickness of more than 1000 metres) is just one of the formations to be found in the beautiful Drakensberg mountain range.*

Drakensberg

Historic Battlefields

*F*or most of the 19th century, the KwaZulu-Natal midlands region was a bloody battlefield, as Zulu, Boer and Briton fought for territorial supremacy. Military enthusiasts will find the Battlefields Route (which includes the sites of Blood River, Isandhlwana, Rorke's Drift, uLundi, Majuba Hill, Talana, Elandslaagte, Tugela Heights, Colenso, Ladysmith and Spioenkop) fascinating. Some of the most dramatic confrontations occurred in the triangular area bounded by Estcourt in the south, Volksrust in the north, and Vryheid to the east.

THE BATTLEFIELDS ROUTE

Blood River (1838): the final and decisive clash between the Zulus and the Voortrekker settlers during the Boer migration into Natal. Raw courage proved no match for superior firepower — more than 3000 Zulus perished on the field; Boer losses amounted to just three wounded.

Isandhlwana (1879): part of a British invading force was annihilated by a 24,000-strong *impi* (army); only a handful

of the 1000-plus redcoats survived.

Rorke's Drift (1879): a bitterly fought skirmish in which a small British garrison held out against wave after wave of Zulu *impi*. Between them, the defenders earned 11 Victoria Crosses.

Majuba Hill (1881): final battle of the brief Anglo-Transvaal war, in which a Boer force of part-time soldiers drove the British regulars from the slopes of the high

hill, inflicting severe casualties. The British commander, Sir George Colley, is thought to have committed suicide during the retreat.

Spioenkop (1900): the Anglo-Boer War's bloodiest battle, savagely fought between Boer and Briton for control of the strategic hill on the route leading to the besieged Ladysmith. Casualties were high on both sides; the Boers eventually prevailed.

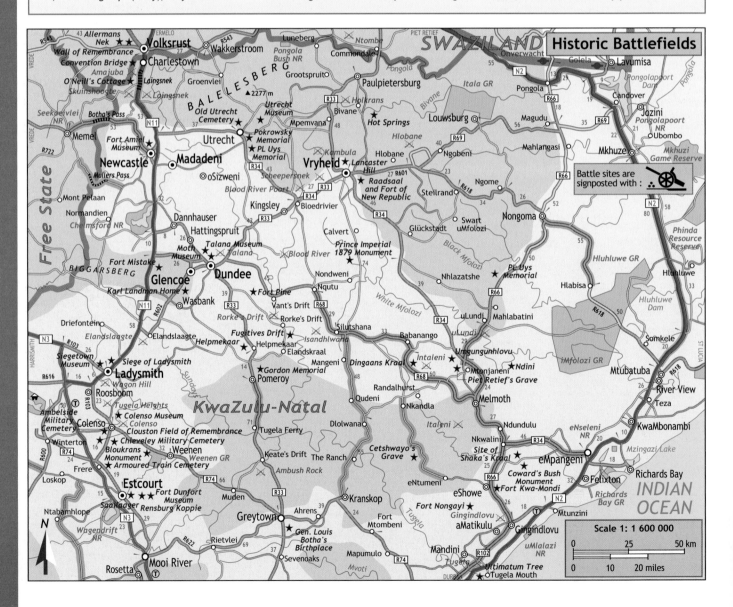

Wild Coast

*S*outhwestwards from the KwaZulu-Natal border lies the Transkei region, its rugged seaboard known as the Wild Coast — an unspoilt and quite beautiful 280km-long (174-mile) wilderness of beaches and secluded bays, lagoons and estuaries (an impressive 18 rivers find their way to the Indian Ocean along the coastal strip), imposing cliffs and rocky reefs that probe, finger-like, out to sea. Rolling green hills and patches of dense vegetation grace the hinterland. Largest of its seaside villages are Port St Johns and Coffee Bay; most prominent resort, the superb Wild Coast Sun.

TRAVEL TIPS

The N2 bisects this region, passing northeast to southwest from Port Shepstone through Kokstad, Mount Frere, Umtata and Butterworth, where grocery supplies and petrol can be obtained. The gravel roads leading down to the coast can be rather taxing on both vehicle and driver. Beware of straying animals.

ACCOMMODATION

Wild Coast Sun and Casino, Transkei region, tel: (039) 305-9111, fax: 305-1012; glitz and glamour.
Trennery's Hotel, tel: (047) 498-0004, fax: 498-0011; beautifully situated on Great Kei River, Kentani district.

Above: *The strange detached cliff known as Hole-in-the-Wall is a well-known spot not far from Coffee Bay on the beautiful Wild Coast.*

MAIN ATTRACTIONS

Wild Coast Sun: an extravagant, luxury hotel-casino complex situated right on the beachfront.
Hole-in-the-Wall: a short drive south of Coffee Bay stands a massive detached cliff with a small arched opening through which the surf thunders.
Mazeppa Bay: palm trees line three wide beaches; the scuba diving, snorkelling and fishing spots are superb.
Qhorha Mouth: a good beach with interesting rock pools, close to the hotel. In the **Dwesa** and **Cwebe nature reserves** buffalo, eland and warthog roam the combined forest and grassland, while crododiles patrol the rivers.
Fishing: catches range from kob, blacktail bronze bream and shad to barracuda and trophy-sized sharks.

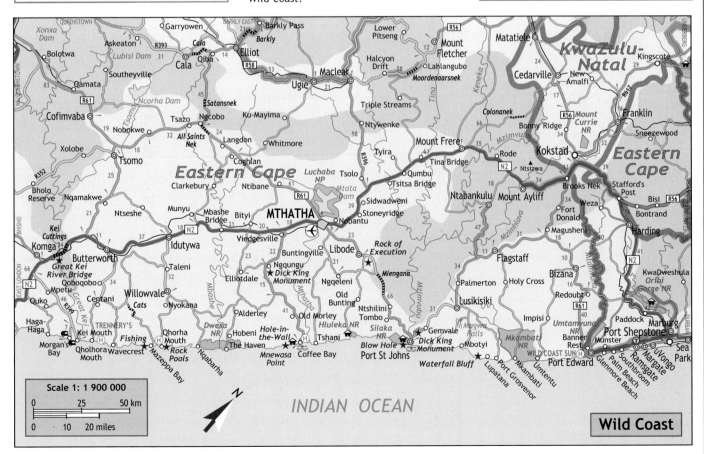

Scale 1: 1 900 000

Wild Coast

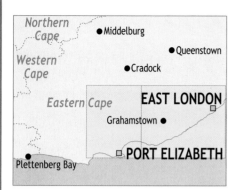

Eastern Cape

The region, extending from the KwaZulu-Natal border and the Wild Coast southwestward, through Algoa Bay, to the lush evergreen Tsitsikamma park, and inland to the foothills of the Drakensberg and the semi-arid edges of the Great Karoo, offers scenic diversity and splendour. The provincial capital is the small town of Bhisho, though Port Elizabeth serves as its economic centre.

ACCOMMODATION

Fish River
Tsolwana Game Reserve, tel: (043) 742-4450; three well-appointed homesteads.
Fish River Sun Hotel, tel: (040) 676-1101; upmarket resort.
Hogsback
Hogsback Inn, tel: (045) 962-1006; beautiful nature walks and prolific bird life.

USEFUL CONTACTS

Nelson Mandela Bay Tourism, tel: (041) 585-8884, fax: 585-2564.
East London Tourism Information, tel: (043) 722-6015, fax: 743-5091.
Grahamstown Tourism Information, tel: (046) 622-3241, fax: 622-3266.
Automobile Association (AA), tel: (086) 111-1994, AA Emergencies: 0800-01-0101, 0800-03-3007, 0800-11-1998.

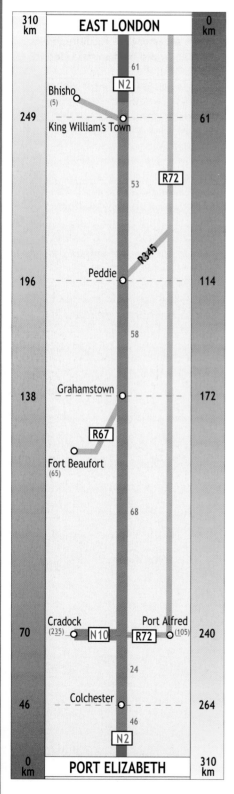

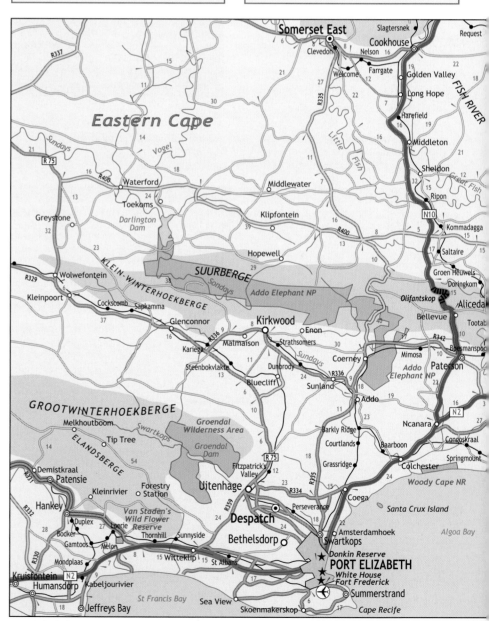

TRAVEL TIPS

The N2 leads west to Cape Town and northeast to Durban. The R32 links Port Elizabeth with Cradock. Wild Coast resorts are accessible via subsidiary (often gravel) roads leading off the N2. When using these roads, beware of potholes, hairpin bends and straying animals.

Right: *Grahamstown is known as the 'City of Saints' for the large number of its churches and as the 'settler city' for its British-colonial origins. For an insight into South African theatre, dance, music, film, fine arts and crafts, don't miss the National Festival of the Arts held in July every year.*

MAIN ATTRACTIONS

Jeffreys Bay: a surfer's paradise.
Grahamstown: academic and cultural centre; hosts acclaimed National Arts Festival each July.
Great Fish River Conservation Area: home to hippo, buffalo and black rhino.
Tsolwana Game Reserve: truly magnificent mountain reserve.
Hogsback: northwest of King William's Town, set among the exquisite forests which provided the inspiration for JRR Tolkien's novel, *The Hobbit*.
Port Alfred: pretty resort town at the mouth of the Kowie River.
Shamwari Game Reserve: the southernmost private big game reserve in Africa — malaria free.

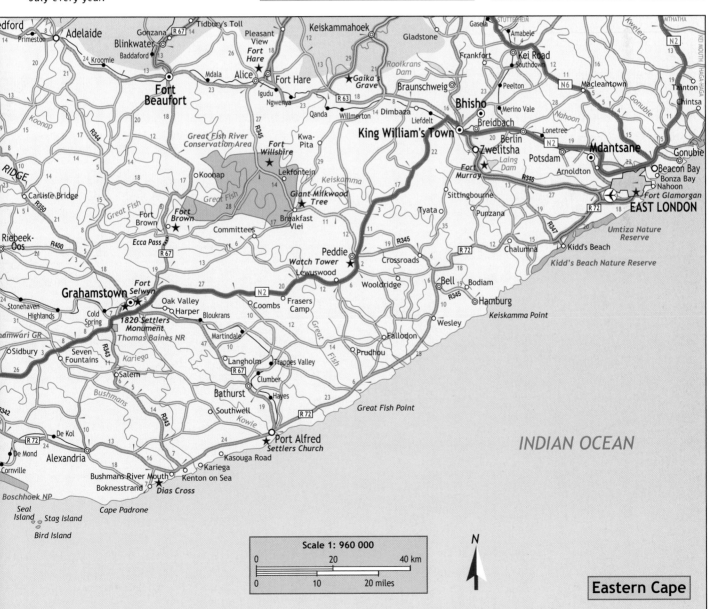

Scale 1: 960 000

0   20   40 km

0   10   20 miles

N

Eastern Cape

Port Elizabeth

Known as the 'friendly city' and also as the 'windy city', Port Elizabeth is the economic hub of the Eastern Cape, much of its industrial activity revolving around the vehicle assembly sector and related enterprises. P.E., as it is most often called, is also a major tourist centre. Set on the shores of Algoa Bay, the country's fifth largest metropolis has some excellent beaches, many historic buildings, sophisticated shopping centres, good hotels and restaurants. Port Elizabeth owes its origins to the 4000 British settlers who landed here in 1820.

MAIN ATTRACTIONS

Beaches: Port Elizabeth has four major beaches: King's, Humewood, Hobie and Pollok, each with its special attractions.

Oceanarium and Museum Complex: at Humewood; see the performing dolphins and seals and visit the Aquarium and Snake Park.

Nature rambles: in and around P.E. lie **St Georges Park** and the **Pearson Conservatory**, **Settlers Park**, the **Island Conservation Area** and the beautifully tended **Van Stadens Wildflower Reserve**.

Addo Elephant National Park: this park, located about 72km (45 miles) northeast of the city, was created in 1931 to protect the few remaining survivors of the once-prolific herds of Cape elephant. The sanctuary offers good game-viewing and comfortable accommodation.

Donkin Heritage Trail: a steeply winding historical walking tour.

Fort Frederick: building of historical significance built in 1799; located on Belmont Terrace, overlooking the Baakens River estuary.

Sardinia Bay: marine reserve with miles of unspoilt coastline and crystal clear water; excellent for diving, horse riding and scenic walks or hikes.

Boardwalk Casino and Entertainment World: family entertainment, shopping, dining and gaming; set around a series of man-made lakes and beautiful gardens lit by 40,000 Tivoli lights.

ACCOMMODATION

Beach Hotel, Humewood, tel: (041) 583-2161, fax: 583-6220; close to Oceanarium and Hobie Beach.

Edward Hotel, tel: (041) 586-2056, fax: 586-4925; Edwardian-style; overlooks Donkin Memorial.

The Humewood, Beach Road, tel: (041) 585-8961, fax: 585-1740; family hotel, attractive rooms.

Formule 1 Hotel, tel: (041) 585-6380, fax: 585-6383; budget.

Protea Lodge, Prospect Hill, tel/fax: (041) 585-1721; budget, Victorian comfort, self-catering.

King's Tide Boutique Hotel: tel: (041) 583-6023, fax: (041) 583-3910; four-star luxury with all amenities, indoor and outdoor entertainment.

USEFUL CONTACTS

St George's Hospital, tel: (041) 392-6111, fax: 392-6000.

Automobile Association, tel: (086) 111-1994.

Computicket, tel: (083) 915-8000.

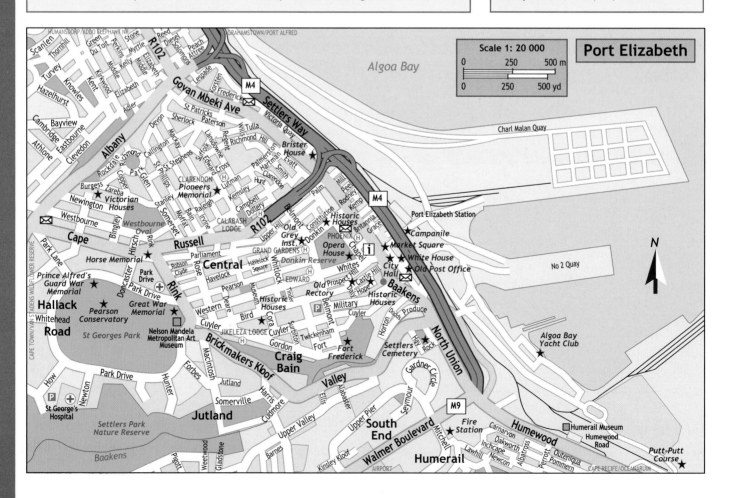

East London

Situated at the mouth of the Buffalo River, the river port of East London combines the charm of a relatively small community with all the essential amenities of a large city. Its attractions are of the quiet, undemanding, family-orientated kind: it has fine beaches, pleasant parks and gardens, good hotels and restaurants, and some entertaining nightlife in the summer months, especially in the seafront area. The principal thoroughfare, Oxford Street, is lined with a variety of modern shops, many of which cater to the tourist trade. The port serves the industries of the Eastern Cape and the Free State.

MAIN ATTRACTIONS

Superb beaches: most popular and accessible is Orient Beach.
East London Museum: Oxford Street; exhibits include the first coelacanth (hitherto thought to be extinct) to be caught and the world's only dodo egg.
Aquarium: over 400 species.
Queens Park Botanical Gardens: splendour of indigenous flora.
Ann Bryant Gallery: fine local paintings and sculptures.
Hiking trails: a choice of walks from the 4-day Shipwreck Trail to the 2-hour Umtiza Trail lead nature lovers along unspoilt beaches, through nature reserves, or into the Amatola mountains to the northwest of East London.
Latimer's Landing: a waterfront development on the banks of the Buffalo River. It offers a variety of restaurants overlooking the small craft anchorage where various boat and yacht rides are offered.

ACCOMMODATION

Blue Lagoon Hotel, Blue Bend Place, Beacon Bay, tel: (043) 748-4821, fax: 748-2037; very close to the beach.
Dolphin View Lodge, Seaview Terrace, tel: (043) 702-8600.
Holiday Inn Garden Court East London, cnr John Bailey and Moore streets, tel: (043) 722-7260, fax: 743-7360; on beachfront, standard rooms, service and value.
Kennaway Hotel, tel/fax: (043) 722-5531; close to the city centre and the beaches, solid value.

Protea Hotel East London, cnr Currie and Inverleith streets, tel: (043) 722-3174.
Windsor Cabanas and Windsor Courtyard, tel/fax: (043) 743-2225; Mediterranean-style, fine views, self-catering option.
The Thatch Guest House, tel: (043) 748-3672, fax: (043) 748-6227; borders an acclaimed bird sanctuary and overlooks the Indian Ocean.
Tidewaters B&B, cell: 082 463 7524, fax: (043) 740-4505; on Gonubie River, with spa.

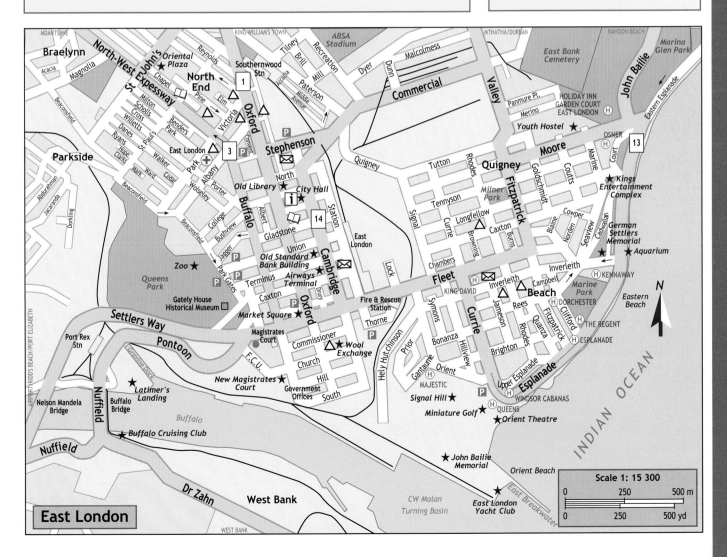

East London

Garden Route

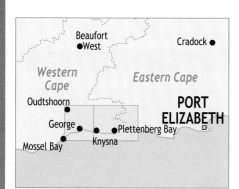

*T*he southern coastal terrace, extending from Humansdorp, the Tsitsikamma and Storms River in the east to Mossel Bay and beyond in the west, is known as the Garden Route. This is an enchanting shoreline of lovely bays and coves, high cliffs and wide estuaries, with a hinterland of mountains, spectacular passes, rivers, waterfalls and wooded ravines. The lagoons and lakes around Knysna and Wilderness are magical stretches of water. The attractions are many: good hotels and eating places, pleasant villages and resorts, and a warm ocean that beckons bather, yachtsman and angler alike. Inland you'll find the town of Oudtshoorn, its surrounding ostrich farms and, to the north, the magnificent Cango Caves.

ACCOMMODATION

Wilderness
Karos Wilderness Hotel,
tel: (044) 877-1110, fax: 877-0600;
surrounded by unspoilt nature;
heated pools.
Fairy Knowe Hotel,
tel: (044) 877-1100, fax: 877-0364;
on the banks of the Touw River.
Palms Wilderness Guest House,
tel: (044) 877-1420, fax: 877-1422.
Knysna
Brenton-on-Sea,
tel: (044) 381-0081, fax: 533-3880;
15km (9 miles) from Knysna.

Plettenberg Bay
Beacon Island Hotel,
tel: (044) 533-1120, fax: 533-3880;
smart, in a unique setting.
Hunter's Country House,
tel: (044) 532-7818; exclusive retreat.
Sedgefield
Lake Pleasant Hotel,
tel: (044) 349-2400, fax: 349-2401;
bass lake.
Oudtshoorn
Riempie Estate Hotel,
tel: (044) 272-6161, fax: 272-6772;
close to Highgate Ostrich Farm.

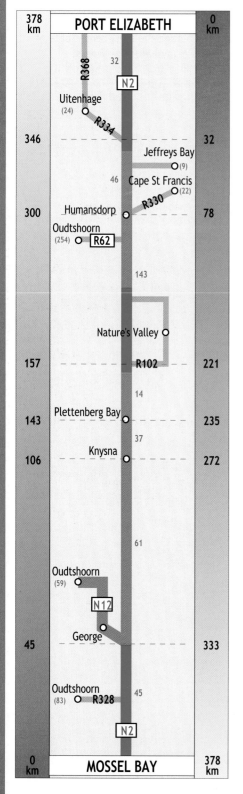

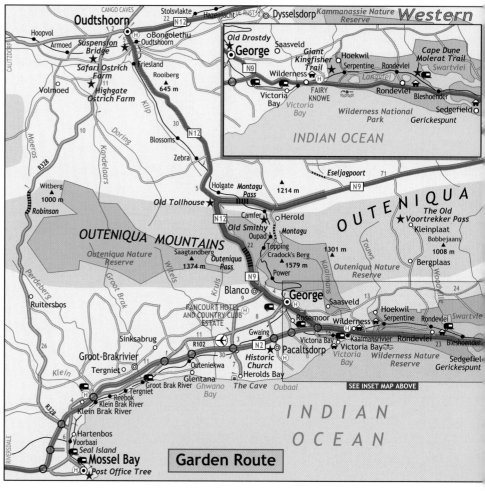

Garden Route

Below: *Hikers on the Tsitsikamma Trail, which winds its way through the park's scenic countryside. Baboon, vervet monkey, honey badger and bushpig are often encountered.*

MAIN ATTRACTIONS

Tsitsikamma National Park and **Otter Trail:** an 80km (50-mile) strip of superb coastline and large offshore marine reserve.

Storms River Mouth: dramatic scenery at this spectacular site; spend a night in the chalets.

Plettenberg Bay: fashionable holiday resort with beautiful beaches.

Mossel Bay: excellent beaches and the Bartolomeu Dias Museum.

Goukamma Nature Reserve: short distance west of Knysna; unspoilt nature and wonderful bird life.

Garden of Eden: a beautiful forest area; many of its trees are labelled.

Knysna: charming little resort town with an attractive lagoon.

Wilderness Lake Area: superb scenery and prolific bird life.

Oudtshoorn: famous for its fascinating ostrich farms.

Cango Caves: complex of caverns ranked among the most remarkable of Africa's many natural wonders.

Bungi jumping: only the brave will attempt the awesome jump off Gouritz River bridge.

USEFUL CONTACTS

Tsitsikamma National Park, tel: (042) 281-1607, fax: 281-1629.
Oudtshoorn Tourism Bureau, tel: (044) 279-2532, fax: 272-8226.
Mossel Bay Tourism Bureau, tel: (044) 691-2202, fax: 690-3077.
Plettenberg Bay Info, tel: (044) 533-4065.

George Tourism Bureau, 124 York Street, tel: (044) 801-9295, fax: 873-5228; tourist information and advice.
Knysna Private Hospital, tel: (044) 384-1083.
Knysna Tourism, tel: (044) 382-5510.

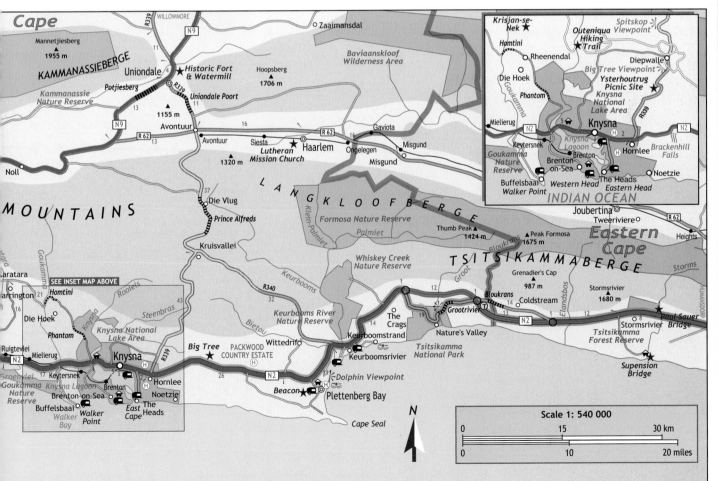

George

*T*his pleasant little city, which was named after England's King George III, lies at the foot of the splendid Outeniqua Mountains and is the Garden Route's principal urban centre. The surrounding countryside is given over to mixed farming, forestry and the cultivation of hops. The town is linked to Knysna by the main Garden Route highway — and by the 'Outeniqua Choo-Tjoe' steam train service.

ACCOMMODATION

Fancourt Hotel and Country Club, tel: (044) 804-0000, fax: 804-0700; elegant accommodation; excellent golfing facilities.
Far Hills Country Hotel, tel: (044) 889-0000, fax: 889-0001; overlooks the Outeniqua Mountains.
Hoogekraal Country House, tel: (044) 879-1277/8, fax: 879-1300; well-kept 18th-century homestead; SATOUR-acclaimed.

MAIN ATTRACTIONS

Outeniqua Choo-Tjoe: this old steam train will take you on a scenic day trip to Knysna, tel: (044) 801-8288.
George Museum: in the Old Drostdy; noted for its antique musical instruments.
Churches: visit St Mark's, South Africa's smallest cathedral; the Dutch Reformed church, completed in 1842; and St Peter and St Paul, the oldest Roman Catholic church in the country.
Beaches: excellent bathing, fishing and sun-worshipping at Herold's and Victoria bays.

Above: *The Outeniqua Choo-Tjoe, an old steam train, offers tourists an especially scenic excursion between Knysna and George.*

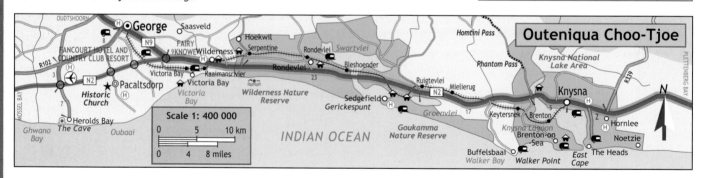

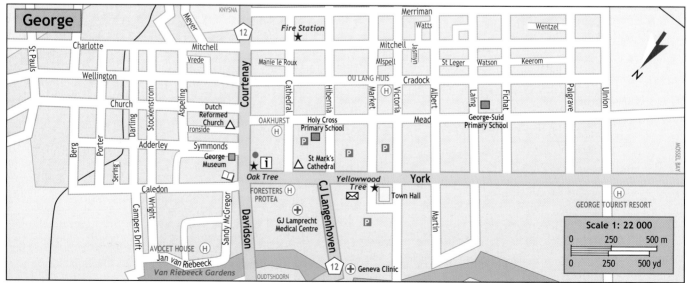

Knysna

*K*nysna is celebrated for its locally brewed draught ale (Mitchell's), its fresh oysters, and the fine furniture made from the area's hardwoods. Its biggest draw-card, however, is Knysna Lagoon: a fine stretch of water guarded by two sandstone cliffs known as The Heads. The lagoon, popular with boating enthusiasts, water-skiers and anglers, harbours a variety of fish and water birds, 'pansy shells' and a rare species of sea horse. Cabin cruisers and houseboats may be hired; the John Benn, a 20-ton pleasure boat, leaves from the jetty each morning (sightseeing, live entertainment, wining and dining on board).

ACCOMMODATION

Belvidere Manor, tel: (044) 387-1055, fax: 387-1059; historic home at the edge of the lagoon; dates back to 1834.
Point Lodge, tel: (044) 382-1944, fax: 382-3455; lake-side, owner-managed, friendly, tranquil setting, *en suite* rooms.
Leisure Isle Lodge, on Ballard Bay, tel: (044) 384-0462, fax: 384-1027; top-rated guesthouse, superb views.
Yellowwood Lodge, tel: (044) 382-5906, fax: 382-4230; owner-managed, friendly, beautiful *en suite* rooms, fine views of lagoon.
Inyathi Guest House, tel: (044) 382-7768, e-mail: info@inyathi-sa.com Individually decorated wooden chalets in the heart of Knysna set in a mostly

indigenous garden. Multilingual owner.
The Russell Hotel, cnr Long, Unity and Graham sts, tel: (044) 382-1058, fax: 382-1083; luxurious hotel centrally situated within walking distance of all Knysna's popular attractions.
Pezula Resort Hotel, Lagoonview Drive, Pezula Estate, tel: Southern Sun Group (011) 679-2994; exclusive cliff-top retreat with its own golf course.
Lightleys Holiday Houseboats, Belvidere Off-ramp, Phantom Pass Road, N2, Belvidere/Brenton, tel: (044) 386-0007, fax 386-0018; catered or self-catered, fully equipped 2-, 4- and 6-berth boats on the safe, tranquil waters of the Knysna Lagoon. Ideal for family holidays or romantic getaways.

MAIN ATTRACTIONS

Knysna Heads: two promontories guarding the entrance to Knysna Lagoon, with good views of the surrounds.
Royal Hotel: Prince Alfred and George Bernard Shaw stayed here.
Millwood Museum: local history, gold mining and timber industry.
Fresh oysters: try some, sprinkled with fresh lemon juice or hot chilli sauce, at the Knysna Oyster Co.
Crab's Creek: a restaurant on the water's edge; sit under umbrellas and enjoy the prolific bird life.
Noetzie: stroll past the five castles overlooking the sea (please note that they are private residences).
Knysna Forest: together with the Tsitsikamma Forest, it forms the largest expanse of indigenous high forest in South Africa.
Elephant Park: educates all ages about the Knysna elephants, tel: (044) 532-7732, fax: 532-7763.
Featherbed Bay Nature Reserve, ferry ride across the bay to the lovely reserve where you can hike, picnic, or dine at the restaurant, tel: (044) 382-1693, fax: 382-2373.

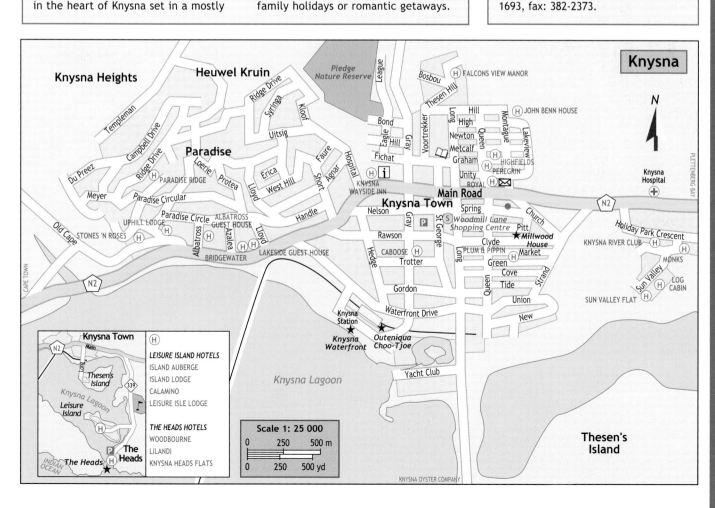

Cape Winelands

Western Cape

Ceres ●
CAPE TOWN ☐
Paarl ●
Stellenbosch ●
Caledon ●

To the north and east of Cape Town is the Winelands, a region of grand mountain ranges, fertile valleys, vineyards and orchards, and of homesteads built in the distinctive and gracious Cape Dutch style. Among its more notable attractions are the various wine routes. Stellenbosch, the country's second oldest urban centre, is the principal town.

MAIN ATTRACTIONS

Stellenbosch: hub of the wineland region; a picturesque university town that prides itself on its lovely historic buildings and oak-lined avenues.

Franschhoek: founded by French Huguenots between 1680 and 1690. Protestant settlers were forbidden to form independent communities and, through intermarriage, lost much of their cultural heritage, but they left an indelible mark on the local wine-growing industry.

Paarl: original farming settlement established in 1720; visit a number of splendid wine estates in the vicinity of this little town.

Somerset West: the beautiful big homestead of Vergelegen estate was built by an early Cape governor and completed in 1701.

Durbanville: situated in peaceful surroundings, the wine estates offer high-quality wines.

USEFUL CONTACTS

Tygerberg Information, Durbanville, tel: (021) 970-3172/3.

Vignerons de Franschhoek (Wine Route), tel: (021) 876-3062/2964.

Franschhoek Tourism Bureau, tel: (021) 876-3603, fax: 876-2768.

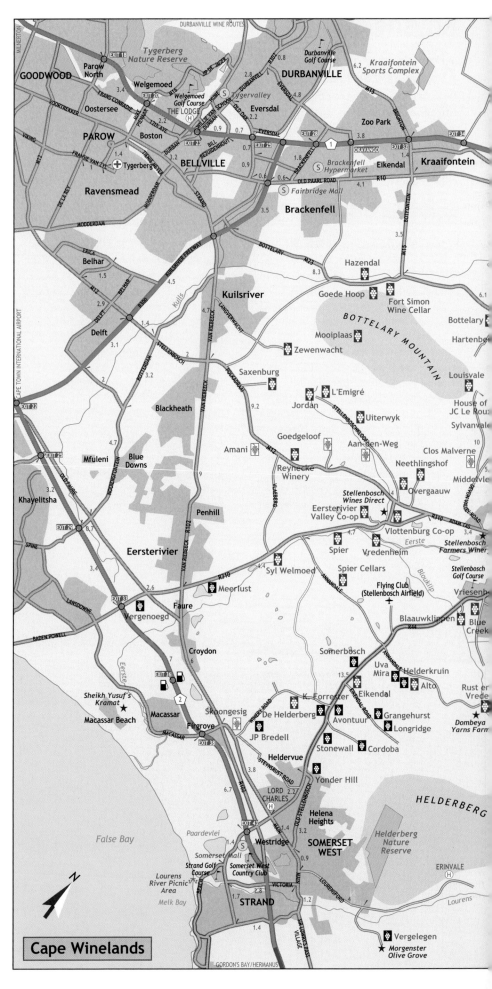

Cape Winelands

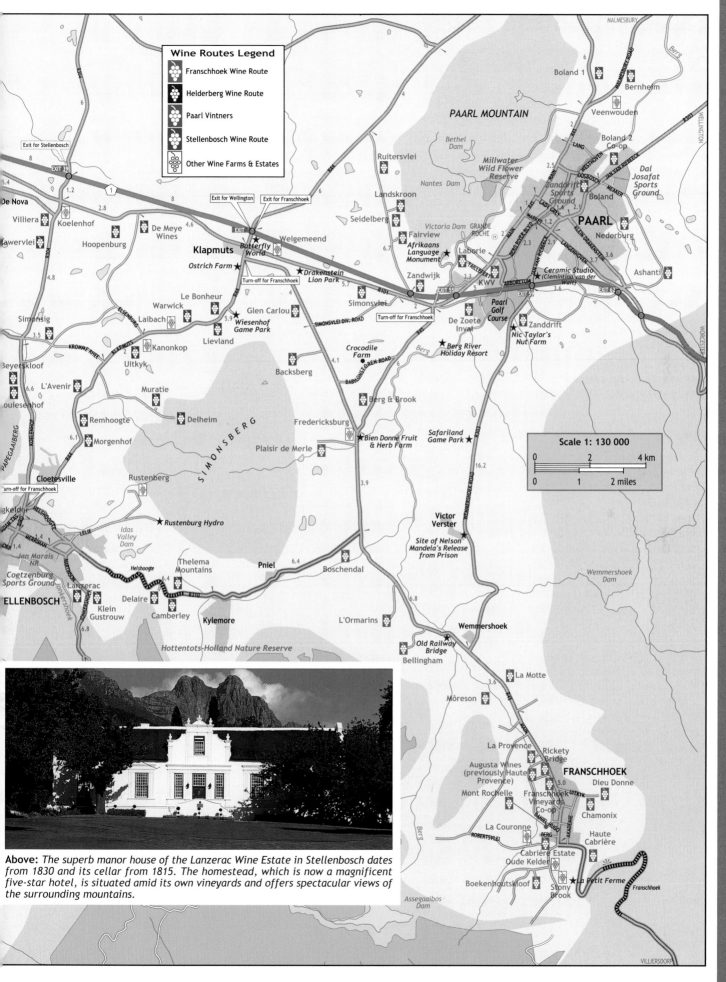

Wine Routes Legend
- Franschhoek Wine Route
- Helderberg Wine Route
- Paarl Vintners
- Stellenbosch Wine Route
- Other Wine Farms & Estates

MALMESBURY

Boland 1

Bernheim

Veenwouden

PAARL MOUNTAIN

Boland 2 Co-op

Dal Josafat Sports Ground

Bethel Dam

Ruitersvlei

Millwater Wild Flower Reserve

Nantes Dam

Zandrift Sports Ground

Boland

PAARL

Landskroon

Victoria Dam   GRANDE ROCHE

Nederburg

Seidelberg

Fairview

Afrikaans Language Monument

Laborie

Ashanti

Exit for Stellenbosch

EXIT 39

De Nova

Villiera

Koelenhof

De Meye Wines

Welgemeend

Klapmuts

Butterfly World

Ostrich Farm

Turn-off for Franschhoek

Drakenstein Lion Park

Zandwijk

KWV

Ceramic Studio (Clemintina van der Walt)

Zanddrift

Exit for Wellington   Exit for Franschhoek

Hoopenburg

Lawervlei

Simonsvlei

De Zoete Inval

Nic Taylor's Nut Farm

Turn-off for Franschhoek

Le Bonheur

Warwick

Wiesenhof Game Park

Glen Carlou

Simonsig

Laibach

Lievland

Berg River Holiday Resort

Paarl Golf Course

Beyerskloof

Kanonkop

Uitkyk

Crocodile Farm

Backsberg

Berg & Brook

L'Avenir

Louiesenhof

Muratie

Delheim

Fredericksburg

Bien Donne Fruit & Herb Farm

Safariland Game Park

Remhoogte

Morgenhof

SIMONSBERG

Plaisir de Merle

Cloetesville

Turn-off for Franschhoek

Rustenberg

Victor Verster

Site of Nelson Mandela's Release from Prison

Wemmershoek Dam

Rustenburg Hydro

Idas Valley Dam

Jan Marais NR

Cogtzenburg Sports Ground

Thelema Mountains

Pniel

Boschendal

Lanzerac

Delaire

Klein Gustrouw

Camberley

Kylemore

L'Ormarins

Wemmershoek

STELLENBOSCH

Old Railway Bridge

Bellingham

La Motte

Môreson

Hottentots-Holland Nature Reserve

Wemmershoek Dam

La Provence

Rickety Bridge

FRANSCHHOEK

Augusta Wines (previously Haute Provence)

Dieu Donne

Mont Rochelle

Franschhoek Vineyards Co-op

Uitkyk

Chamonix

La Couronne

Haute Cabrière

Cabrière Estate

Oude Kelder

Boekenhoutskloof

Stony Brook

La Petit Ferme

Franschhoek

Assegaaibos Dam

VILLIERSDORP

Scale 1 : 130 000

0   2   4 km

0   1   2 miles

Above: *The superb manor house of the Lanzerac Wine Estate in Stellenbosch dates from 1830 and its cellar from 1815. The homestead, which is now a magnificent five-star hotel, is situated amid its own vineyards and offers spectacular views of the surrounding mountains.*

Stellenbosch and Paarl

South Africa's second oldest urban centre and heart of the Winelands, Stellenbosch lies in a pleasant valley, less than an hour's drive from Cape Town. Founded in 1669, the settlement matured gracefully over the centuries, its broad thorough-fares lined by stately oaks and splendid historic buildings. It is the hub of an enchanting wine route and a leading seat of learning, home to a major university and several respected schools. Paarl, the biggest of the region's towns, began in 1720 as a farming and wagon-building centre, taking its name from the pearl-like cluster of granite rocks atop the overlooking mountain.

ACCOMMODATION

Grande Roche Hotel, tel: (021) 863-2727, fax: 863-2220; elegant hotel with award-winning Bosman's Restaurant.

Lanzerac Manor and Winery, tel: (021) 887-1132, fax: 887-2310; superb facilities, elegantly refurbished; wine made on the premises.

D'Ouwe Werf, tel: (021) 887-4608, fax: 887-4626; tradition and atmosphere combined.

Roggeland Country House, tel: (021) 868-2501, fax: 868-2113; internationally acclaimed.

USEFUL CONTACTS

Stellenbosch Wine Route office, tel: (021) 886-4310/30.
Stellenbosch Information Office, tel: (021) 883-3584, fax: 883-8017.
Paarl Vintners, tel: (021) 863-4886.
Paarl Tourism Bureau, tel: (021) 863-4937.

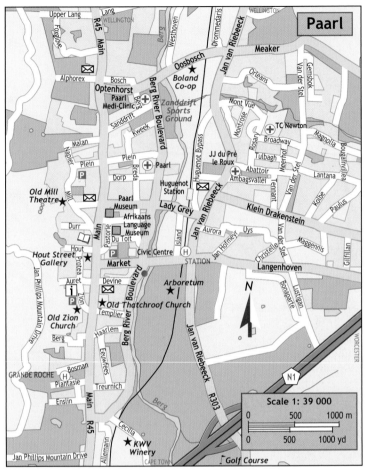

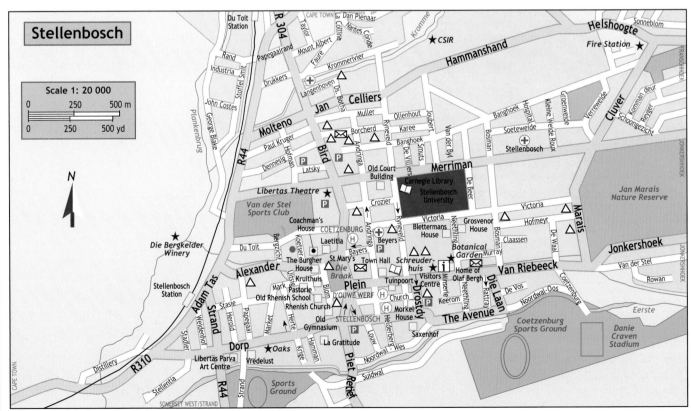

West Coast

The western shores of the country, pounded by the cold Atlantic Ocean, are a rather barren region of low coastal vegetation. Sleepy fishing villages bake in the sun, while inland small farming communities huddle together in the vast emptiness. But the area is transformed after the spring rains, when a carpet of flowers erupts in a riot of colour stretching as far as the eye can see.

MAIN ATTRACTIONS

West Coast National Park: beautiful natural wetland reserve with prolific **bird life** and magnificent wild flowers each spring (August–October). The **Flowerline** provides useful information about the best displays, tel: (083) 910-1028.

Langebaan Lagoon: a 16km-long (10-mile) inlet, the focal point of the park and a paradise for bird-watchers, anglers, and water-sports enthusiasts.

Club Mykonos, a splendid Greek-style leisure and accommodation complex, is located nearby.

Above: *After the spring rains, the parched land lies resplendent in a colourful tapestry of flowers.*

ACCOMMODATION

Protea Saldanha Bay,
51 Main Street, Saldanha, tel: (022) 714-1264, fax: 714-4093.
Lambert's Bay Hotel,
tel: (027) 432-1126, fax: 432-1036; a comfortable and friendly establishment.

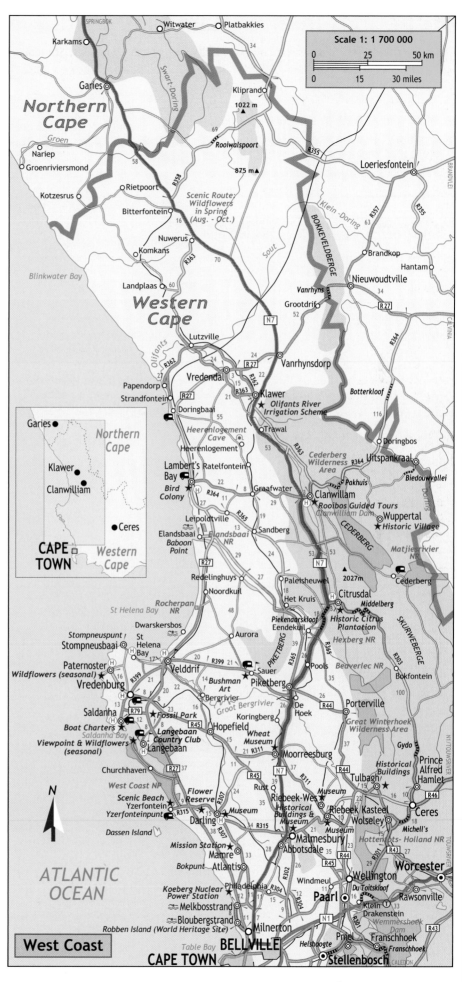

Cape Peninsula

The Cape Peninsula stretches from the Cape of Good Hope and Cape Point northward to Table Bay and comprises, for the most part, a strikingly beautiful plateau that achieves its loftiest and most spectacular heights in the famed Table Mountain massif overlooking Table Bay and Cape Town — a neat, bustling metropolis of handsome buildings, elegant thoroughfares and glittering shops. The Peninsula's western seaboard is scenically superb, its eastern shoreline graced by excellent beaches and attractive residential and resort centres that are a magnet for holiday-makers, scuba divers, boating enthusiasts, surfers and sun-worshippers.

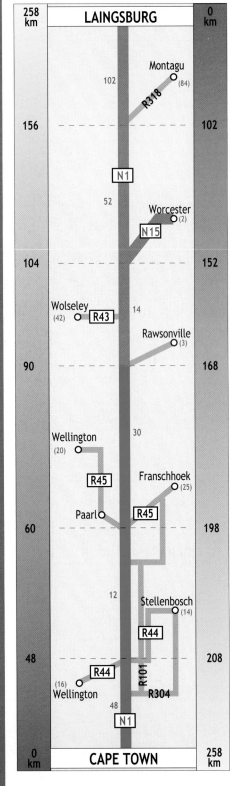

ACCOMMODATION

Protea Hotel Sea Point, tel: (021) 434-1187, fax: 434-3597; comfortable accommodation.

Peninsula All-Suite Hotel, Sea Point, tel: (021) 430-7777, fax: 430-7776; on the promenade.

Alphen Hotel, tel: (021) 794-5011, fax: 794-5710; charming wine estate in Constantia Valley.

Holiday Inn Garden Court Newlands, tel: (021) 683-6562, fax: 683-6794; close to the Newlands cricket ground and rugby stadium.

The Vineyard Hotel, Newlands, tel: (021) 657-4500, fax: 657-4501; historic country house.

The Lord Nelson Inn, Simon's Town, tel: (021) 786-1386, fax: 786-1009; colonial-style inn offering old-fashioned hospitality.

Quayside Resort, Simon's Town, tel: (021) 786-3838, fax: 786-2241; luxury hotel, waterfront setting.

Lord Charles Hotel, Somerset West, tel: (021) 855-1040, fax: 855-1107; gracious elegance; world-class.

TRAVEL TIPS

Rail, bus and taxi services are adequate. Major international car-hire companies are represented, as are local car, camper, and caravan-hire firms. Tour operators offer a wide choice of one-day and half-day scenic coach trips. Please note: South African taxis must be booked or boarded at the designated stands, as they do not cruise for fares.

Above: *A cable car takes visitors up to the lookout at Cape Point for panoramic views of False Bay and the southern Atlantic Ocean.*

MAIN ATTRACTIONS

Cape Town: this charming metropolis is set beneath the majesty of Table Mountain. *See page 49.*

Table Mountain: *see page 49.*

Kirstenbosch: *see page 48.*

The V&A Waterfront: *see page 52.*

Chapman's Peak Drive: a world-renowned scenic route.

Clifton: chic suburb noted for its four magnificent beaches; popular with the trendier set.

Hout Bay: enchanting little suburb with a quaint fishing harbour.

Cape Point: southernmost tip of the Peninsula; the finest of view sites.

Robben Island: *see* page 53.

Simon's Town: the headquarters of the South African Navy, noted for its proximity to the fine beaches of Seaforth, as well as the African penguin colony at Boulders. For details, see www.simonstown.com

Constantia Wine Estates: five estates in the Constantia Valley: Groot and Klein Constantia, Buitenverwachting, Steenberg and Uitsig. Contact Groot Constantia for information, tel: (021) 794-5128; fax: (021) 794-1999.

Ratanga Junction: Africa's first full-scale theme park; family entertainment, tel: 0861 200 300.

GrandWest Casino: situated in Goodwood, includes gaming rooms, eateries and an olympic-size ice-rink, tel: (021) 505-7777, fax: 505-7656.

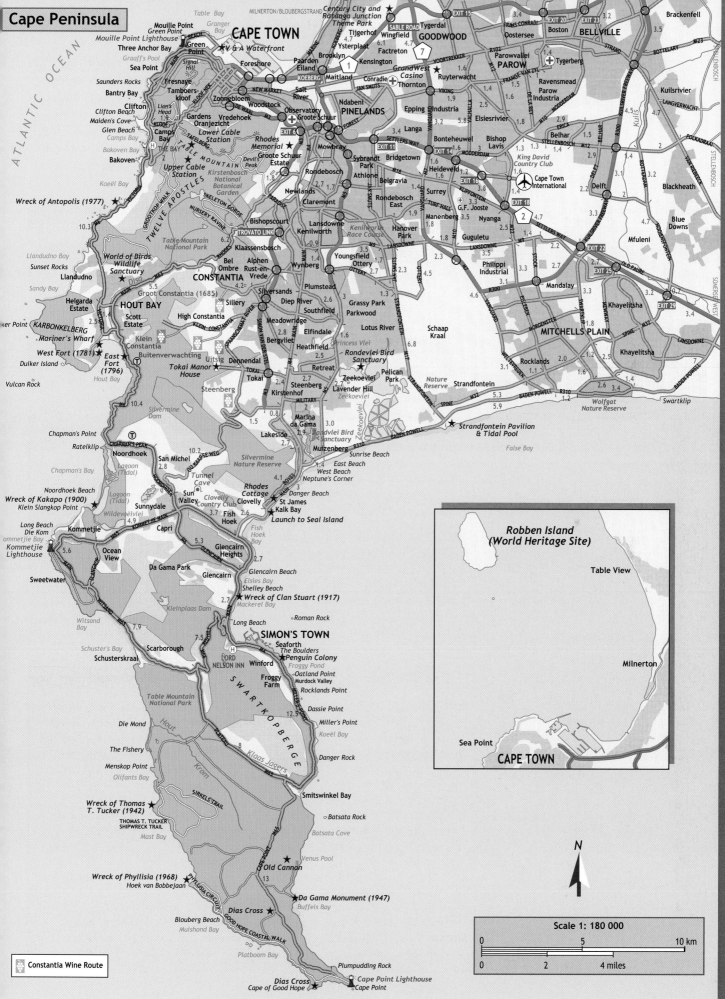

Cape Peninsula

Kirstenbosch

*T*he Kirstenbosch National Botanical Garden lies on the eastern slopes of the Table Mountain range. An astonishing array of flowering plants, representative of about a quarter of South Africa's 24,000 species, is cultivated here. Delightful walks lead through herb and fragrance gardens, and through stinkwood and yellowwood groves. There is a pelargonium koppie and a cycad amphitheatre, and the bird life, particularly the sunbirds drawn to the wealth of proteaceae, is enchanting. The Botanical Society Conservatory enables Kirstenbosch to display South African plants which cannot be grown in the outdoor gardens.

Above: *The rugged east face of the Table Mountain massif frames the delicate beauty of Kirstenbosch.*

ENCHANTED GARDEN

Braille walk/fragrance garden: designed especially for blind visitors.
Visitor's Centre, tel: (021) 799-8782. A glass conservatory and relaxing restaurant.
Van Riebeeck's hedge: part of the original wild almond hedge planted by the first Dutch settlers centuries ago.
Compton Herbarium: contains over 200,000 plant specimens.
Sunday music concerts: sundowner picnics in summer.
Kirstenbosch Garden, tel: (021) 799-8783, www.sanbi.org

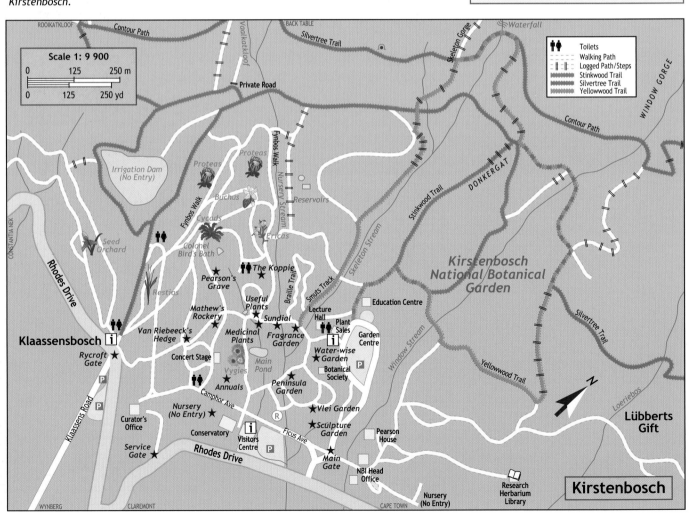

Cape Town

*T*he central metropolitan area of Cape Town huddles in a 'bowl' formed by Table Mountain, its flanking peaks and the broad sweep of Table Bay. Founded by Dutch settlers in 1652, this is the country's oldest city and fourth largest in terms of population. More than 300 years of history have created its unique architectural character — a vibrant blend of Dutch, French, English and Malay influences. It is an attractive, colourful city that boasts excellent hotels and restaurants, open-air markets and shops catering for every pocket and taste. The central area is small, compact, and easily explored on foot.

MAIN ATTRACTIONS

Table Mountain: ride the cable car or hike to the summit, and enjoy the breathtaking views.
Castle of Good Hope: the city's most notable edifice (built between 1666 and 1679).
Victoria and Alfred Waterfront: *see* page 52.
St George's Cathedral: visit the famous Rose Window over the south transept in this lovely church.
Greenmarket Square: for bargain hunting in one of Africa's prettiest little plazas. Be sure not to miss the **Old Town House** (built 1761) which contains the Michaelis collection of 17th-century Dutch and Flemish art, tel: (021) 481-3933.
The Company Gardens: take a walk through the lush gardens founded by Jan van Riebeeck. While here, visit the South African Museum (tel: 481-3800),

Planetarium and National Art Gallery.
Koopmans De Wet House: admire the beautiful antique furniture, tel: (021) 481-3935.
Bargains: Cape Town's informal markets are the place to shop for contemporary African art, curios, ethnic jewellery and more. Try St George's Mall, Greenmarket Square and the Kirstenbosch Craft Market.
Rhodes Memorial: a grandiose monument with breathtaking views, located on the eastern slopes of Devil's Peak; lovely restaurant.
Signal Hill: have a sundowner and enjoy the panoramic view.
Bo-Kaap Museum: dedicated to the Malay culture; in one of the oldest original buildings, tel: (021) 481-3939.
Cape Town Holocaust Centre: the only holocaust centre in Africa, tel: (021) 462-5553, fax: 462-5554.

ACCOMMODATION

The Bunkhouse, 23 Antrim Road, Three Anchor Bay, tel/fax: (021) 434-5695; budget accommodation.
The Cape Milner Hotel, 2a Milner Rd, Tamboerskloof, tel: (021) 426-1101, fax: 426-1109; conveniently close to town.
Cellars-Hohenort Hotel, Constantia, tel : (021) 794-2137, fax: 794-2149; built 1693; lovely grounds; excellent restaurant.
The Cullinan Hotel, Cullinan Street, tel: (021) 418-6920, fax: 418-3559; centrally located; excellent service.
Mount Nelson, Gardens, tel: (021) 483-1000, fax: 483-1782; one of the world's most elegant hotels.
Holiday Inn Cape Town, tel: (021) 488-5100, fax: 423-8875; city centre; excellent restaurants.
Park Inn, Greenmarket Square, tel: (021) 423-2050, fax: 423-2059; charming position in the heart of town.
Protea Hotel President, Bantry Bay, tel: (021) 434-8111, fax: 434-9991; luxurious, exquisitely sited on a rocky seafront.

Below: *The arrival of the strong southeasterly wind is heralded by the appearance of the famous 'tablecloth' over Table Mountain.*

EVENTS AND FESTIVALS

Minstrel Carnival: vibrant part of the **New Year** celebrations.
Metropolitan Handicap (J&B): horse-racing event held in **January**.
Spring Wildflower Show: held at Kirstenbosch in **September**.
Cape Argus Pick 'n Pay Cycle Tour: held on the second **Sunday** of **March**.
Two Oceans Marathon: this popular event takes place on **Easter Saturday**.

USEFUL CONTACTS

Cape Town Tourism, tel: (021) 426-4260.
Groote Schuur Hospital, tel: (021) 404-9111.
Table Mountain Aerial Cableway Co Ltd, tel: (021) 424-8181.
Castle of Good Hope, tel: (021) 787-1500, fax: 787-1133.

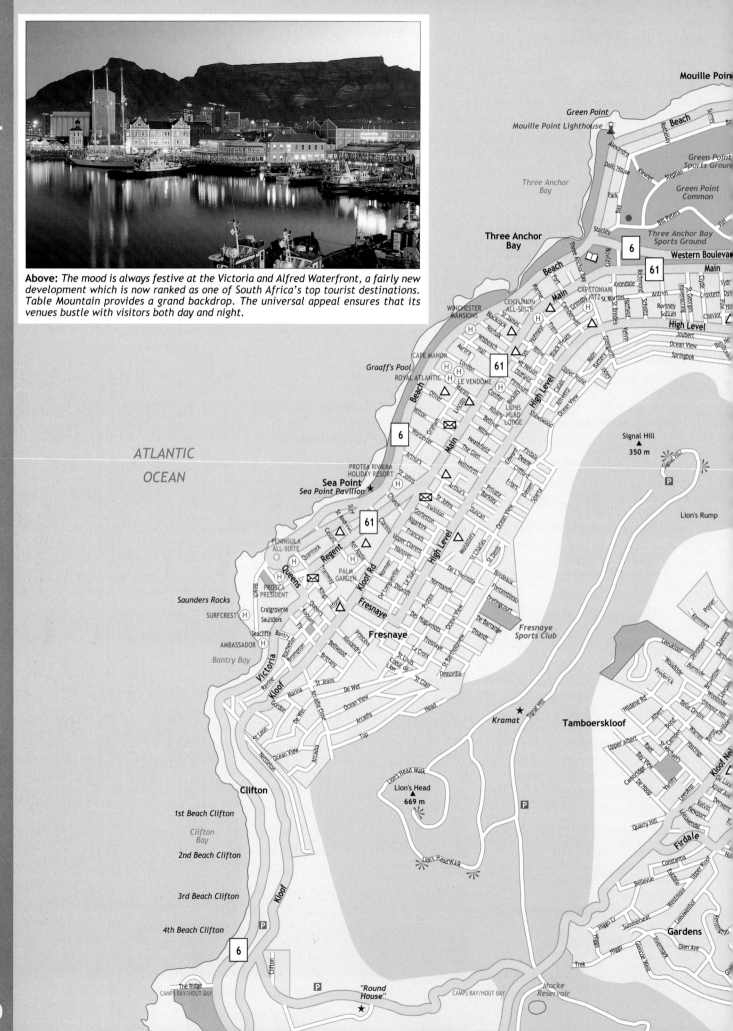

Above: *The mood is always festive at the Victoria and Alfred Waterfront, a fairly new development which is now ranked as one of South Africa's top tourist destinations. Table Mountain provides a grand backdrop. The universal appeal ensures that its venues bustle with visitors both day and night.*

ATLANTIC
OCEAN

Mouille Point

Green Point
Mouille Point Lighthouse
Beach
Three Anchor Bay
Green Point Sports Ground
Green Point Common
Three Anchor Bay
Western Boulevard
Three Anchor Bay Sports Ground
Beach
WINCHESTER MANSIONS
CENTURION ALL-SUITE
Main
CAPETONIAN
High Level
Main
CAPE MANOR
Graaff's Pool
ROYAL ATLANTIC
LE VENDOME
LIONS HEAD LODGE
High Level
Signal Hill
350 m
Lion's Rump
PROTEA RIVIERA HOLIDAY RESORT
Sea Point
Sea Point Pavilion
High Level
PENINSULA ALL-SUITE
Regent
Queens
PALM GARDEN
Kloof Rd
PROTEA PRESIDENT
Fresnaye
Saunders Rocks
SURFCREST
Craigrownie
Saunders
Seacliffe
AMBASSADOR
Bantry Bay
Fresnaye
Fresnaye Sports Club
Tamboerskloof
Kramat
Signal Hill
Clifton
1st Beach Clifton
Clifton Bay
2nd Beach Clifton
Lion's Head
669 m
Lion's Head Walk
3rd Beach Clifton
Firdale
4th Beach Clifton
Gardens
The Ridge
CAMPS BAY/HOUT BAY
"Round House"
CAMPS BAY/HOUT BAY
Mocke Reservoir

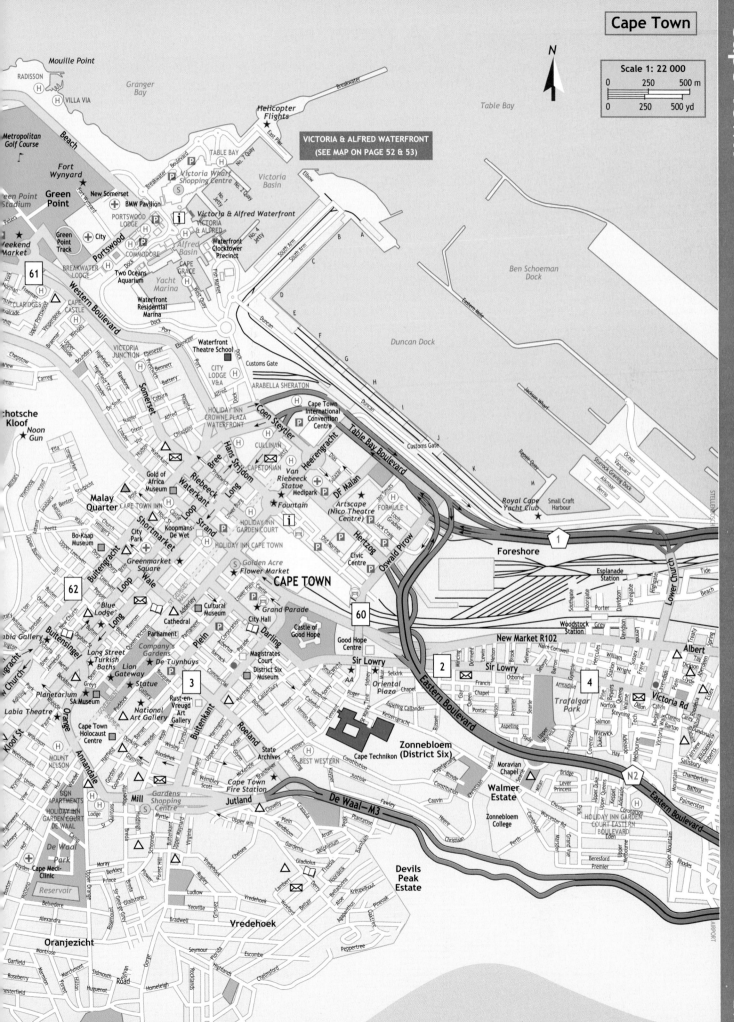

V & A Waterfront

After a long separation, city and harbour are once again happily reunited through the ambitious Victoria and Alfred Waterfront redevelopment scheme, a multi-billion-rand private venture that borrowed ideas from the successful harbour projects of New York, Vancouver and Sydney among others, yet retains a sparkling, lively character of its own.

A Difficult Choice

The Hildebrand: elegant, cosy dining.
Morton's on the Wharf: Cajun-Creole.
Den Anker: top-class Belgian cuisine.
Belthazar: delicious seafood.
Ocean Basket: variety of seafood.
Quay 4: restaurant and tavern.

Accommodation

The Table Bay Hotel, tel: (021) 406-5000, fax: 406-5686; elegant luxury; modern convenience.
Cape Grace Hotel, tel: (021) 410-7100, fax: 419-7622; on the West Quay, spectacular views.
Victoria and Alfred Hotel, tel: (021) 419-6677, fax: 419-8955; Victorian elegance alongside the Alfred Basin; great view of Table Mountain.
Victoria Junction Hotel, Somerset Road, Green Point, tel: (021) 418-1234, fax: 418-5678; avant-garde; loft-style Art Deco.
City Lodge Waterfront, tel: (021) 419-9450, fax: 419-0460; convenient location at main entrance to the Waterfront.

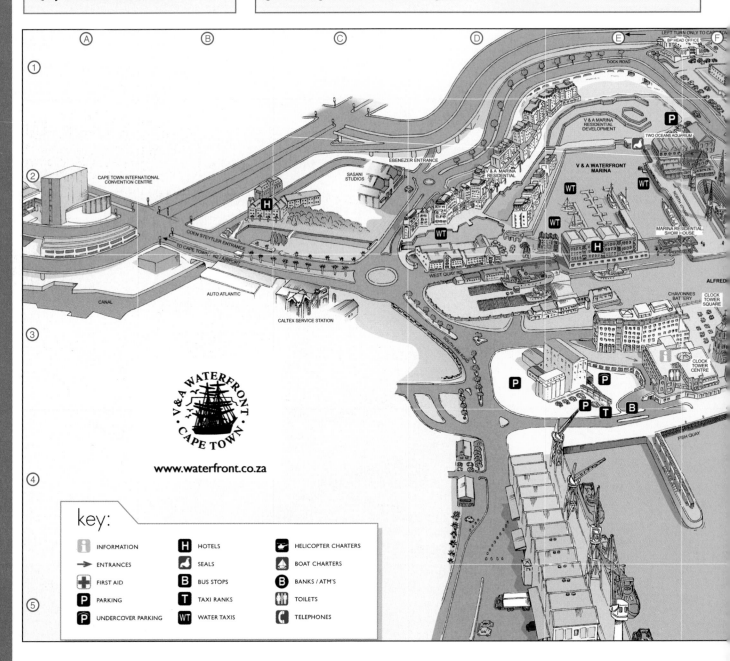

www.waterfront.co.za

key:

i INFORMATION	**H** HOTELS	HELICOPTER CHARTERS
➜ ENTRANCES	SEALS	BOAT CHARTERS
+ FIRST AID	**B** BUS STOPS	**B** BANKS / ATM'S
P PARKING	**T** TAXI RANKS	TOILETS
P UNDERCOVER PARKING	**WT** WATER TAXIS	TELEPHONES

MAIN ATTRACTIONS

Two Oceans Aquarium: an imaginative 35 million-rand complex of world-class standard; watch shoals of fish swim through giant aquariums and explore the touch pools.

South African Maritime Museum: on 4000m^2 (13,123ft^2); the largest display of model ships in South Africa. There is also a discovery cove for the children.

SAS *Somerset*: explore this interesting floating exhibit.

Art and Craft Market: filled with an enormous variety of goods that will appeal to both young and old.

The *Victoria*: a floating treasure museum that exhibits artefacts salvaged from ships wrecked along the coast of the Cape of Storms.

The King's Warehouse: sample the fare of the many diverse food stalls and shop at the huge fish market.

The Red Shed: watch artists at work as they create a variety of items, from delicate glass-blown flowers to colourful ethnic oil paintings and wooden toys.

Cape fur seals: a thriving, wild community of these mammals frequents the calm harbour waters. Watch them diving, lazily floating around, or basking in the sun.

Boat trips: a number of boats and smaller vessels are available for harbour and sunset cruises, as well as longer trips to historic **Robben Island**, the former prison enclave whose most famous inmate was Nelson Mandela.

Concerts: often held at the Amphitheatre; an event calendar is available from information kiosks.

Shops and restaurants: plenty of options to choose from with 400 shops, 70 eateries and extended opening hours.

Spring Flower Show: landscaping, gardening and flower exhibition, flower carpet, show gardens, floral art displays, a photographic exhibition and a Flower Power Concert; from 3 to 7 September.

Air Charters & Tours, The Hopper: NAC Makana Aviation offer Cape Town's only helicopter experience with single seats. Flights depart from the Waterfront; includes spectacular views of the city, Robben Island, Lion's Head, Table Mountain and surrounds. www.waterfront.co.za

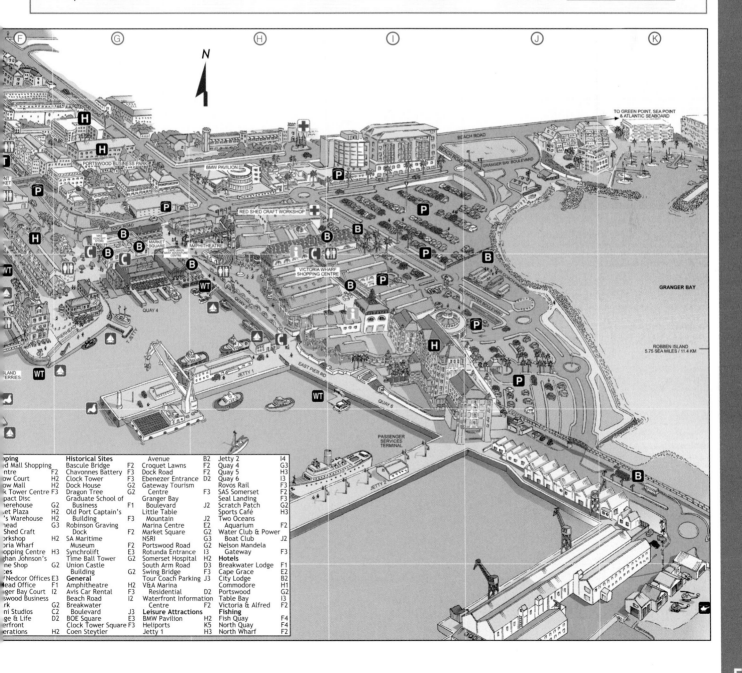

Shopping		Historical Sites		Avenue	B2	Jetty 2	I4
...d Mall Shopping		Bascule Bridge	F2	Croquet Lawns	F2	Quay 4	G3
...ntre	F2	Chavonnes Battery	F3	Dock Road	F2	Quay 5	H3
...ow Court	H2	Clock Tower	F3	Ebenezer Entrance	D2	Quay 6	I3
...ow Mall	H2	Dock House	G2	Gateway Tourism		Rovos Rail	I3
...k Tower Centre	F3	Dragon Tree	G2	Centre	F3	SAS Somerset	F2
...pact Disc		Graduate School of		Granger Bay		Seal Landing	F3
...erehouse	G2	Business		Boulevard	F1	Scratch Patch	G2
...et Plaza	H2	Old Port Captain's		Little Table		Sports Café	H3
...'s Warehouse	H2	Building	F3	Mountain	J2	Two Oceans	
...head	G3	Robinson Graving		Marina Centre	E2	Aquarium	F2
... Shed Craft		Dock	F2	Market Square	G2	Water Club & Power	
...orkshop	H2	SA Maritime		NSRI	G3	Boat Club	J2
...oria Wharf		Museum	F2	Portswood Road	G2	Nelson Mandela	
...opping Centre	H3	Synchrolift	E3	Rotunda Entrance	I3	Gateway	F3
...han Johnson's		Time Ball Tower	G2	Somerset Hospital	H2		
...ne Shop	G2	Union Castle		South Arm Road	D3	**Hotels**	
...es		Building	G2	Swing Bridge	F3	Breakwater Lodge	F1
...Nedcor Offices	E3	**General**		Tour Coach Parking	J3	Cape Grace	E2
...ead Office	F1	Amphitheatre	H2	V&A Marina	E2	City Lodge	B2
...ger Bay Court	I2	Avis Car Rental	F3	Residential	D2	Commodore	H1
...swood Business		Beach Road	I2	Waterfront Information		Portswood	G2
...rk	G2	Breakwater		Centre	F3	Table Bay	I3
...ni Studios	C2	Boulevard	J3	**Leisure Attractions**		Victoria & Alfred	F2
...ge & Life	D2	BOE Square	E3	BMW Pavilion	H2	**Fishing**	
...erfront		Clock Tower Square	F3	Heliports	K5	Fish Quay	F4
...erations	H2	Coen Steytler		Jetty 1	H3	North Quay	F4
						North Wharf	F2

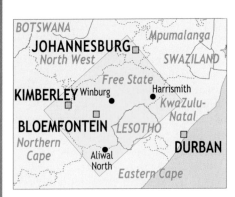

Free State

This rather dry, mostly flat and largely treeless east-central region of South Africa offers the visitor a number of appealing destinations, from game reserves teeming with a variety of wildlife to the evocative Bushman rock paintings along the eastern escarpment. Mine dumps greet your arrival at towns like Welkom, Allanridge and Virginia, all of which have grown up around the goldfields that were opened up shortly after World War II.

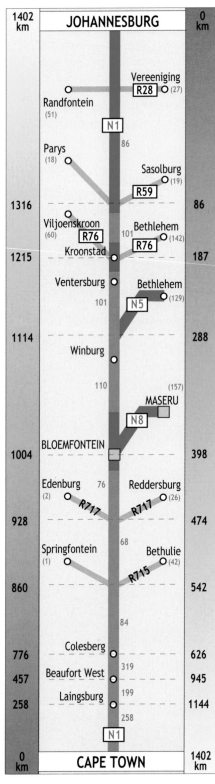

MAIN ATTRACTIONS

Bloemfontein: attractive and vibrant capital of the Free State.

Maria Moroka Nature Reserve: a pleasant mountain reserve, near the small town of **Thaba 'Nchu** and sanctuary for antelope and other wildlife; splendid scenery.

Golden Gate Highlands National Park: scenic wildlife reserve with dramatically sculpted sandstone ridges and cliffs.

The Vaal Dam: 300km² (116-sq-mile) stretch of water, popular with boating enthusiasts and fishermen.

Willem Pretorius Nature Reserve: game reserve between Winburg and Ventersburg; variety of wildlife including white rhino, giraffe and buffalo; tel: (057) 652-2200.

Gariep Dam: the country's largest water reservoir; near Bethulie.

Gariep Dam Nature Reserve: located on the vast dam's northern shore; home to a very large population of graceful springbok.

ACCOMMODATION

Thaba 'Nchu Sun Hotel and Casino Complex, tel: (051) 871-4200, fax: 873-2521; some 75km (47 miles) east of Bloemfontein.

Welkom Inn, Welkom, tel: (057) 357-3361, fax: 352-1458.

Gariep Dam Hotel, Gariep Dam, tel: (051) 754-0060, fax: 754-0268.

Hacienda Hotel, Kroonstad, tel: (056) 212-5111, fax: 213-3298.

Below: This visually bare landscape, near Kroonstad, is typical of the Free State. Here, a rain-laden sky dominates the great, undulating grasslands, punctuated by a solitary windmill.

TRAVEL TIPS

The Free State's main roads are in good condition, linking this central region with other major South African cities. Please note: distances between towns are vast, so be sure to fill up with petrol regularly.

USEFUL CONTACTS

Universitas Hospital, Bloemfontein, tel: (051) 405-3911, fax: 444-0792.

Bloemfontein Publicity, tel: (051) 405-8111/448-8795.

Kimberley Information Centre, tel: (053) 832-7298, fax: 832-7211.

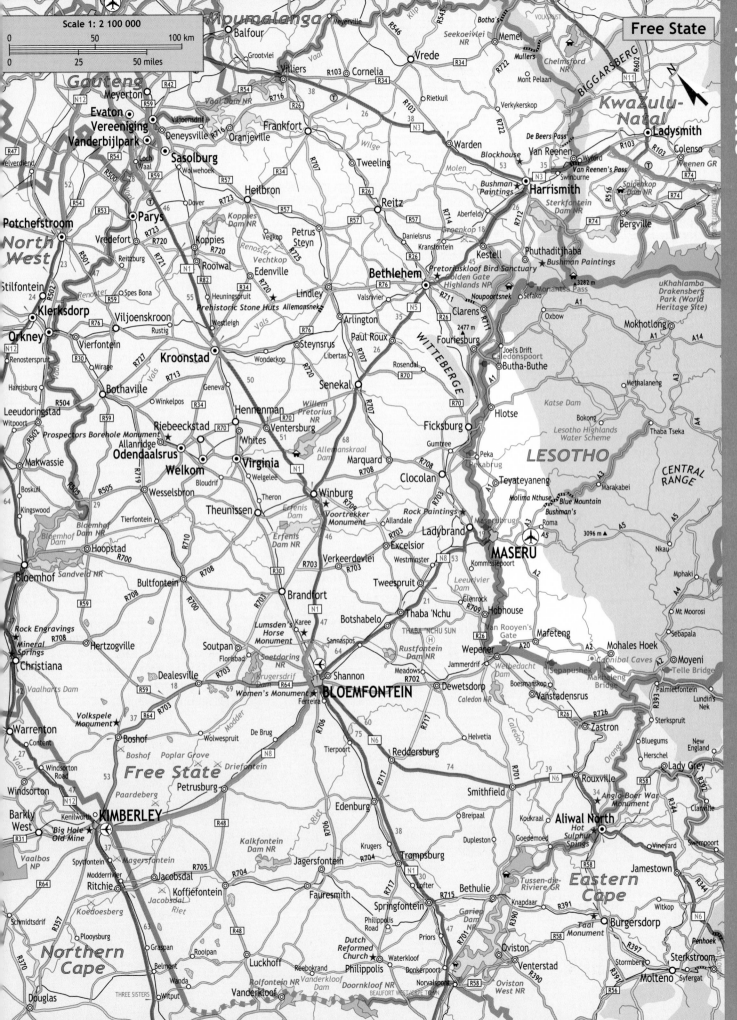

Bloemfontein

Bloemfontein is the judicial capital of South Africa and the principal city of the Free State. The most centrally situated of South Africa's major cities, it lies at the heart of an area of fertile farmland 1392m (4567ft) above sea level and owes much of its prosperity to the Free State goldfields, located 160km (100 miles) to the northeast. The city is noted for its impressive old buildings, museums, monuments, memorials and public parks and gardens.

MAIN ATTRACTIONS

Franklin Nature Reserve: on Naval Hill; home to a variety of wildlife.

National Botanical Garden: pleasant floral sanctuary dominated by impressive dolomite outcrops.

Orchid House: pools, waterfalls and over 3000 exquisite orchids at the foot of Naval Hill.

The Waterfront (Loch Logan): also visit the zoo and the rose garden.

National Women's Memorial: in memory of the more than 27,000 Boer women and children who died in British concentration camps during the Anglo-Boer War.

The Old Raadsaal: the old town hall, housed in a lovely building.

Sand du Plessis Theatre: modern complex; the splendid works of art contribute to the decor.

Soetdoring Nature Reserve: on the R64 to Kimberley; protective habitat for antelope, lion, cheetah and brown hyena.

National Afrikaans Literary Museum: in the Old Government Building; a treasure house of African literature, with manuscripts, etc., belonging to well-known South African writers. Also houses the Afrikaans Music Museum (musical instruments) and Theatre Museum.

ACCOMMODATION

Holiday Inn Garden Court, tel: (051) 444-1253.
Landmark Lodge Protea Hotel Bloemfontein, East Burger Street, tel: (051) 403-8000, fax: 447-7102.
Premier Protea Hotel, 202 Nelson Mandela Drive, tel: (051) 444-4321.
President Hotel, tel: (051) 430-1111, fax: 430-4141; at the foot of Naval Hill.

TRAVEL TIPS

Bloemfontein is on the main north-south highway, the N1, which links Cape Town to Johannesburg. Good tarred roads connect the city with all the surrounding major centres, such as Welkom (R700 and R710); Kimberley (R64); Maseru in Lesotho (R64); and East London on the coast (R30).

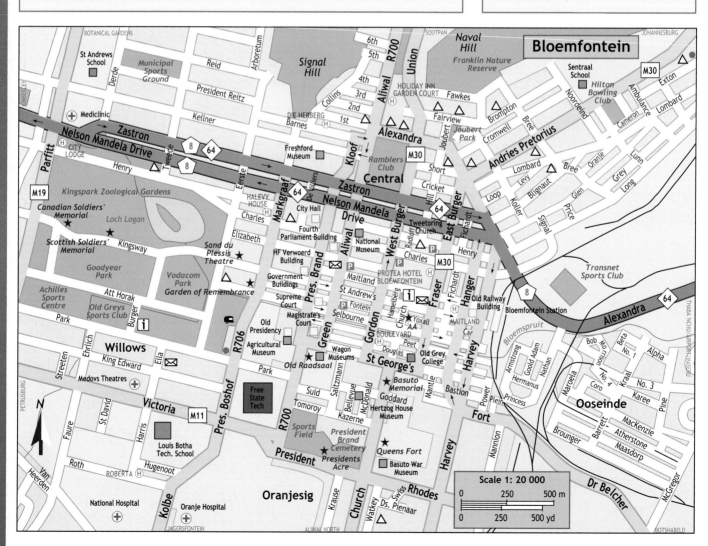

Kimberley

*K*imberley, the world-renowned diamond centre and capital of neighbouring Northern Cape province, was born in the 1870s when tens of thousands of prospectors poured into the area to unearth the glittering gems that lay in abundance beneath the dusty ground. Kimberley still retains much of the old-world atmosphere of these heady days, when instant fortunes were made (and lost), and money and champagne flowed like water.

Accommodation

Holiday Inn Garden Court Kimberley, tel: (053) 833-1751, fax: 832-1814; lovely garden setting.
Hotel Kimberlite, tel: (053) 831-1968; within easy walking distance of the Big Hole.
Horseshoe Motel, Memorial Road, tel/fax: (053) 832-5267.

Right: *When diamond fever struck in 1871, no one could have guessed that 43 years later the Big Hole would reach a depth of 1097m (3600ft). Between 1871 and 1914, 22.6 million tons of earth was excavated from the mine for a yield of 2722kg (6000lb) of diamonds.*

Main Attractions

The Big Hole: Kimberley's historic hub. By the time it was closed in 1914 it had yielded almost three tons of diamonds.
Kimberley Mine Museum: evocative and comprehensive insight into the town's lively past.
Duggan-Cronin Gallery: an outstanding photographic display of the San-Bushman culture.
William Humphreys Gallery: an excellent collection of South African and European paintings, sculpture and furniture.
The Diggers Fountain: honours the miners who helped to build the Diamond City.
Magersfontein battlefield: for directions, call tel: (053) 833-7115.
Star of the West: this public house was the favorite rendezvous of diamond prospectors from the early 1870s. Has a stool said to have been made specially for Cecil Rhodes.

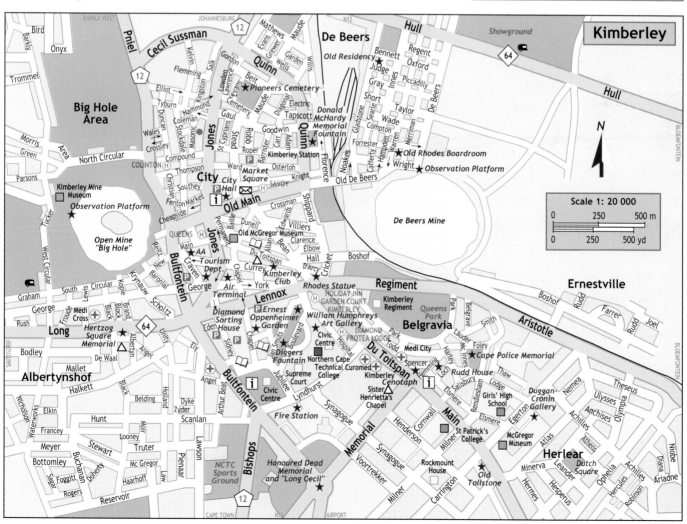

Main Map Section Key and Legend

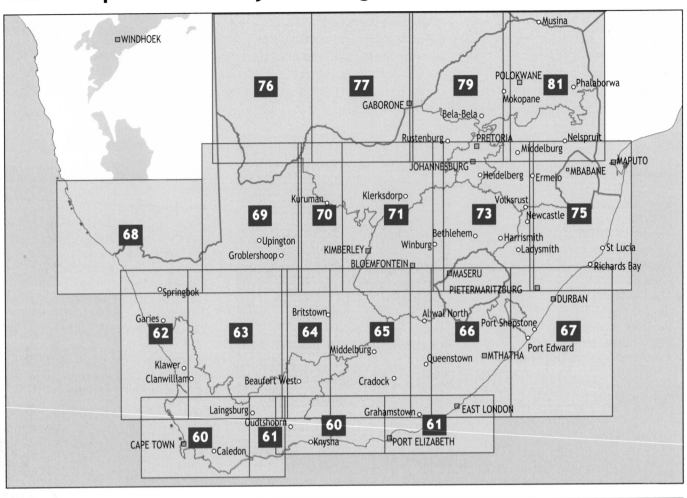

Pages 60-61
Scale 1: 1 790 000

| 0 | 50 | 100 km |
| 0 | 25 | 50 miles |

Pages 62-81
Scale 1: 1 600 000

| 0 | 50 | 100 km |
| 0 | 25 | 50 miles |

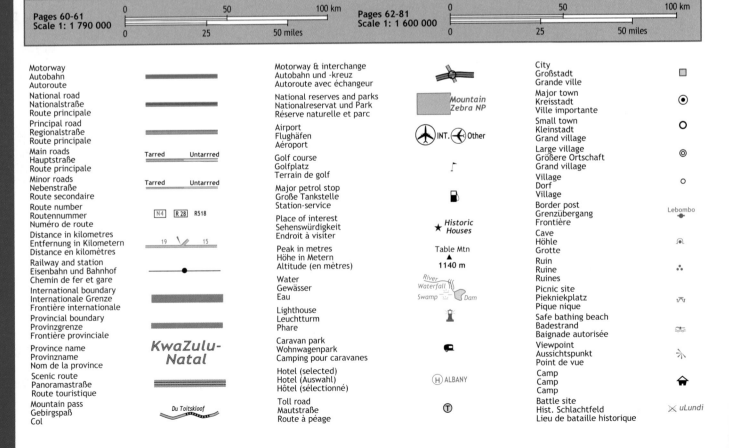

Motorway
Autobahn
Autoroute

National road
Nationalstraße
Route principale

Principal road
Regionalstraße
Route principale

Main roads
Hauptstraße
Route principale — Tarred / Untarrred

Minor roads
Nebenstraße
Route secondaire — Tarred / Untarrred

Route number
Routennummer
Numéro de route — N4 R 28 R518

Distance in kilometres
Entfernung in Kilometern
Distance en kilomètres — 19 / 15

Railway and station
Eisenbahn und Bahnhof
Chemin de fer et gare

International boundary
Internationale Grenze
Frontière internationale

Provincial boundary
Provinzgrenze
Frontière provinciale

Province name
Provinzname
Nom de la province — *KwaZulu-Natal*

Scenic route
Panoramastraße
Route touristique

Mountain pass
Gebirgspaß
Col — *Du Toitskloof*

Motorway & interchange
Autobahn und -kreuz
Autoroute avec échangeur

National reserves and parks
Nationalreservat und Park
Réserve naturelle et parc — *Mountain Zebra NP*

Airport
Flughäfen
Aéroport — INT. / Other

Golf course
Golfplatz
Terrain de golf

Major petrol stop
Große Tankstelle
Station-service

Place of interest
Sehenswürdigkeit
Endroit à visiter — ★ *Historic Houses*

Peak in metres
Höhe in Metern
Altitude (en mètres) — ▲ Table Mtn 1140 m

Water
Gewässer
Eau — *River / Waterfall / Swamp / Dam*

Lighthouse
Leuchtturm
Phare

Caravan park
Wohnwagenpark
Camping pour caravanes

Hotel (selected)
Hotel (Auswahl)
Hôtel (sélectionné) — Ⓗ ALBANY

Toll road
Mautstraße
Route à péage — Ⓣ

City
Großstadt
Grande ville

Major town
Kreisstadt
Ville importante

Small town
Kleinstadt
Grand village

Large village
Größere Ortschaft
Grand village

Village
Dorf
Village

Border post
Grenzübergang
Frontière — Lebombo

Cave
Höhle
Grotte

Ruin
Ruine
Ruines

Picnic site
Piekniekplatz
Pique nique

Safe bathing beach
Badestrand
Baignade autorisée

Viewpoint
Aussichtspunkt
Point de vue

Camp
Camp
Camp

Battle site
Hist. Schlachtfeld
Lieu de bataille historique — ✕ *uLundi*

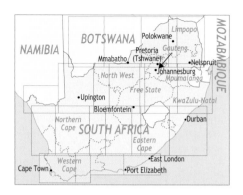

Eastern and Western Cape

Dominated by series after series of soaring mountain ranges interspersed with rolling wheat fields, orchards and vineyards, the southern part of South Africa is one of the continent's most beautiful regions. Inland there are forests, deep fertile valleys and spectacular mountain passes to explore, while the rugged, rocky coastline offers the visitor countless venues for safe bathing, surfing, beachcombing and fishing, together with a number of delightful holiday villages and towns. So gloriously abundant is the flora of this particular stretch of South African coastline that it has been named the Garden Route.

MAIN ATTRACTIONS

Wineland towns: wide, tree-lined avenues and historic buildings.
Day drives: along the southern coastline; two are particularly recommended: from Cape Town to the little town of Hermanus, haven for southern right whales; and from Cape Town to Langebaan Lagoon on the West Coast, renowned for its bird life.
The Garden Route: from Mossel Bay to the Storms River, scenically one of the

most splendid parts of the South African coastline; visit the towns of Knysna and Plettenberg Bay.
Hex River Valley: dramatic sandstone crags dominate the green, beautiful valley, where excellent grapes are cultivated.
The Little Karoo: a beautiful and rugged region lying between the southern coastal rampart and the Swartberg uplands to the north.

TRAVEL TIPS

The N2 national route leads eastward along the south coast from Cape Town to East London, and is the best way to see

the beautiful South African countryside. The road is wide and in excellent condition and petrol stations are frequent.

Below: A myriad vineyards have been established in the fertile soils of the beautiful Hex River Valley.

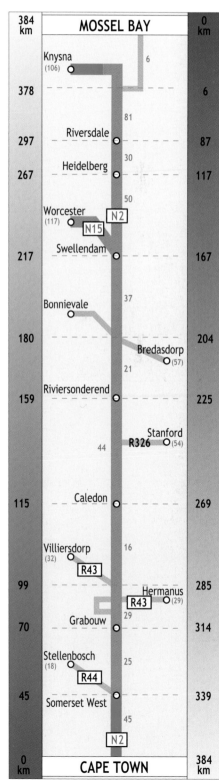

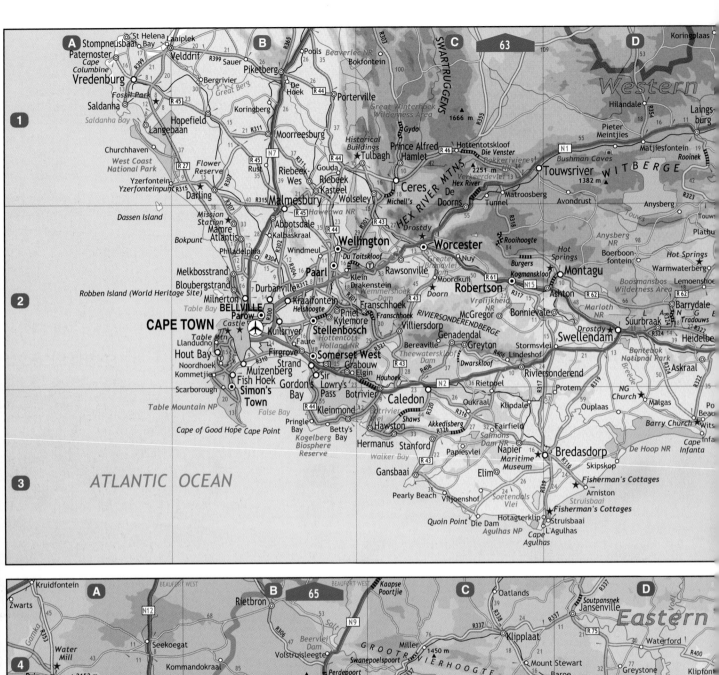

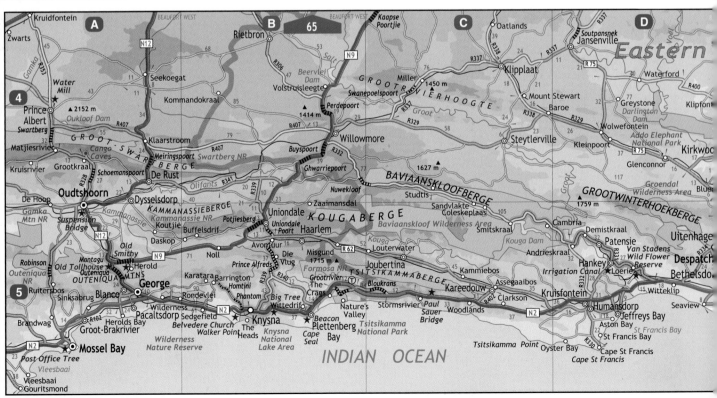

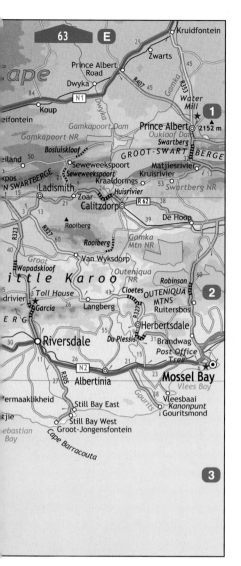

Above: *The scenic splendour of Knysna Lagoon has ensured the resort town's popularity, and the lagoon is lined with many attractive homes and holiday retreats in garden settings.*

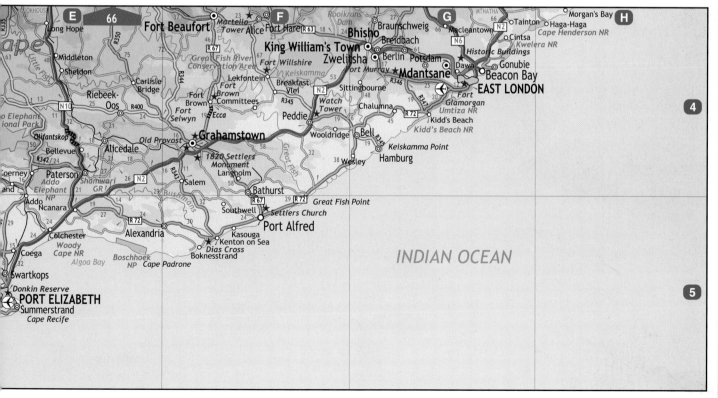

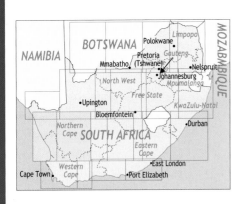

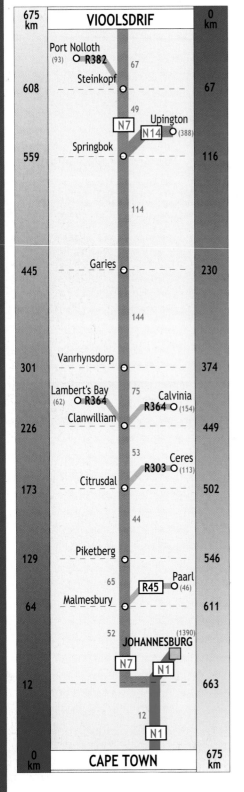

675 km	VIOOLSDRIF	0 km
	Port Nolloth (93) ○ **R382**	
		67
608	Steinkopf	67
	49	
	N7 Upington **N14** (388)	
559	Springbok	116
	114	
445	Garies	230
	144	
301	Vanrhynsdorp	374
	Lambert's Bay (62) ○ **R364**	75 Calvinia **R364** (154)
226	Clanwilliam	449
	53	
	R303 Ceres (113)	
173	Citrusdal	502
	44	
129	Piketberg	546
	65 **R45** Paarl (46)	
64	Malmesbury	611
	52	
	JOHANNESBURG (1390)	
	N7 **N1**	
12		663
	12	
	N1	
0 km	**CAPE TOWN**	675 km

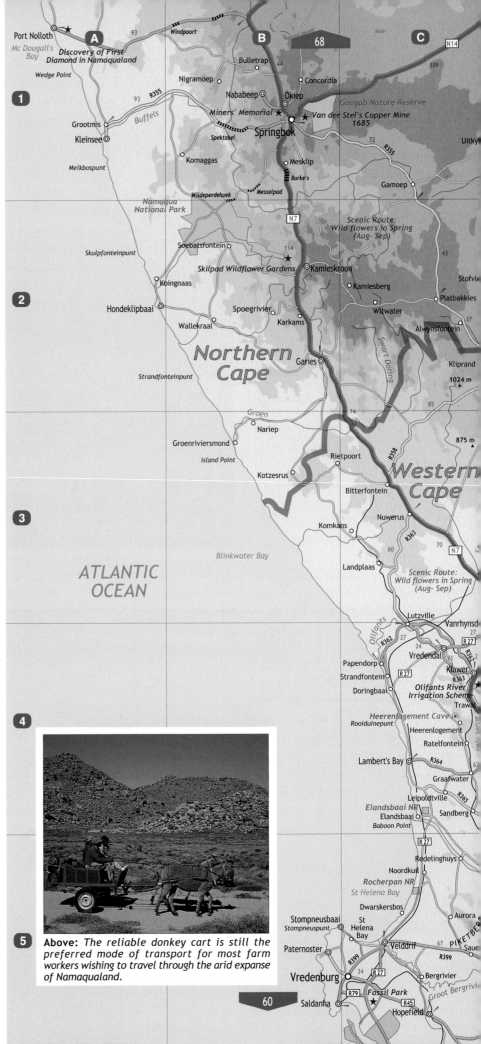

Above: *The reliable donkey cart is still the preferred mode of transport for most farm workers wishing to travel through the arid expanse of Namaqualand.*

Great Karoo

This semi-arid region of bone-dry air, minimal rainfall and intense sunshine dominates the Cape interior. The countryside stretches endlessly to the distant horizons, dotted with lonely windmills and isolated farmsteads.

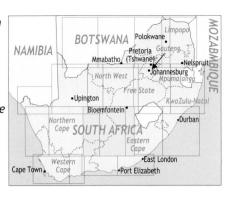

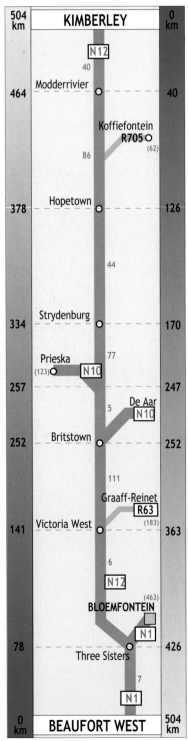

504 km	**KIMBERLEY**	0 km
	N12	
	40	
464	Modderrivier	40
	Koffiefontein R705	
86		(62)
378	Hopetown	126
	44	
334	Strydenburg	170
	77	
257	Prieska (123) N10	247
	De Aar 5 N10	
252	Britstown	252
	111	
	Graaff-Reinet R63	
141	Victoria West (183)	363
	6	
	N12	
	BLOEMFONTEIN (463)	
	N1	
78	Three Sisters	426
	7	
	N1	
0 km	**BEAUFORT WEST**	504 km

MAIN ATTRACTIONS

Beaufort West: birthplace of the famed heart surgeon Chris Barnard; this little town is also noted for its lovely, pear-tree-lined streets.

Karoo National Park: north of Beaufort West; wildlife includes mountain zebra, shy leopard and antelope.

Graaff-Reinet: third oldest town in the Cape, with some fine old architecture.

Valley of Desolation: near Graaff-Reinet; a fantasia of wind-eroded, strangely shaped dolerite peaks, pillars and balancing rocks.

Nieu-Bethesda: tiny hamlet, 50km (31 miles) north of Graaff-Reinet; home to the Owl House Museum's bizarre sculptures, many of which are decorated with ground glass.

Cradock: in the vicinity are the Mountain Zebra National Park and author Olive Schreiner's grave.

Aliwal North: this pleasant town to the far east of the Great Karoo has hot sulphur springs and an excellent spa.

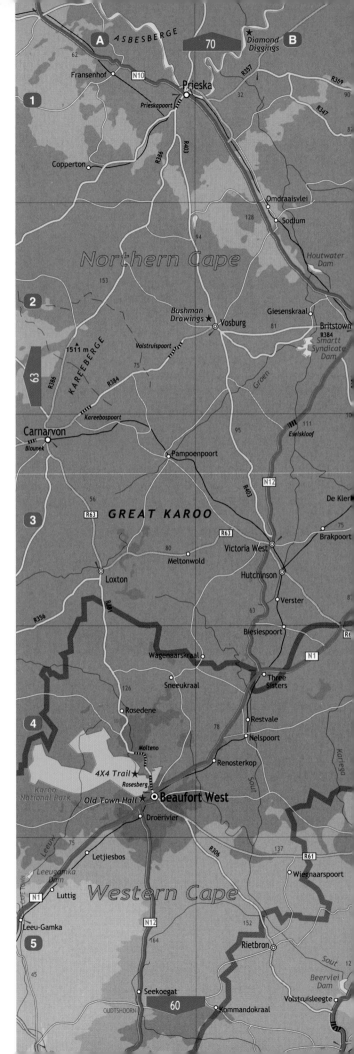

Redcliffe
Rosetta **ESTCOURT**
Nottingham Road
Kamberg
iMpendle
Howick
Hilton
PIETERMARITZBURG
Edendale
Thornville
Bulwer
Richmond
Donnybrook
Creighton
Bush Reserve
KwaZulu-Natal
iXopo
Umzimkulu
Highflats
Harding
Weza
Bizana
Impisi
Redoubt
Munster
Ramsgate
Southbroom
Glenmore Beach
Port Edward
Banner Rest
Umtentu
Mkambati Nature Reserve
Mkambati
South Sand Bluff
Port Grosvenor
Mbotyi

Eastern Cape

New Hanover
Dalton
Mpolweni
VALLEY OF 1000 HILLS
Ndwedwe
Hammarsdale
Krantzkloof NR
Mpumalanga
Rosebank
St Faith's
KwaDweshula
Oribi Gorge NR
Marburg
Sea Park
uMtentweni
Port Shepstone
uVongo
Margate
Paddock

Tugela Mouth
Darnall
Stanger
Groutville
Shakaskraal
Tongaat
iNanda
Verulam
uMhlanga
KwaMashu
DURBAN
Pinetown
Queensburgh
uMlazi
iSipingo
uMbogintwini
Kingsburgh
aManzimtoti
uMgababa
uMkomaas
uMzinto
Scottburgh
Park Rynie
Sezela
Mtwalume
Hibberdene

★ **Ultimatum Tree**
Fort Pearson
★ Shaka's Memorial
Blythdale Beach
Salt Rock
Shaka's Rock
Ballito
The Bluff

INDIAN OCEAN

NAMIBIA
BOTSWANA
MOZAMBIQUE
Limpopo
Polokwane
Pretoria (Tshwane)
Nelspruit
Maftkeng
Gauteng Johannesburg
Mpumalanga
North West
Upington
Free State
Bloemfontein
KwaZulu-Natal
Durban
Northern Cape
Eastern Cape
East London
Western Cape
Cape Town
Port Elizabeth

Above: *The wide mouth of the Mgeni River, in Durban, is spanned by several bridges. The renowned Mgeni River Bird Park, which houses some 300 exotic and local species and is rated the third best in the world, is accessible via the Mgeni River Bridge from the Marine Parade.*

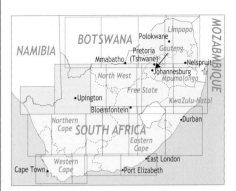

Northern Cape

Much of this region — the western part — is a dry, rather forbidding moonscape of low mountains and strange plants like the kokerboom. After the rainy season, however, the arid veld is transformed into a riot of colour as wild flowers bloom in abundance. Towns are few and small, with the exception of Upington, which is beautifully situated along the banks of the Orange River.

TRAVEL TIPS

The main highways that service the northern and northwestern Cape, and those which traverse the vast Karoo region, are generally in good condition. Note: be sure to stop for petrol and refreshments in good time, as the towns (and the service stations) tend to lie rather far apart in this region. Beware of wild animals crossing the road, especially at dawn, dusk and at night.

MAIN ATTRACTIONS

Upington: visit one of the dried fruit co-ops around the town.
Augrabies Falls National Park: marvel at the lovely waterfall (one of the five biggest in the world) in this otherwise harsh area, and drive through the reserve to spot the bird- and wildlife.
Kgalagadi Transfrontier National Park: straddles the South Africa-Botswana border north of Upington. This is the first of Africa's 'peace parks'. The red sand dunes of the southern segment, shy Kalahari lion, an abundance of raptor species, and magnificent sunsets attract nature lovers to this unique desert park.
Goegab Nature Reserve: east of Springbok; spot eland, springbok and mountain zebra along hiking trails and game drives.
Richtersveld National Park: in the far northwestern corner of the province; hauntingly beautiful.
Vioolsdrif/Noordoewer: South Africa-Namibia border post, for travellers heading to Namibia.

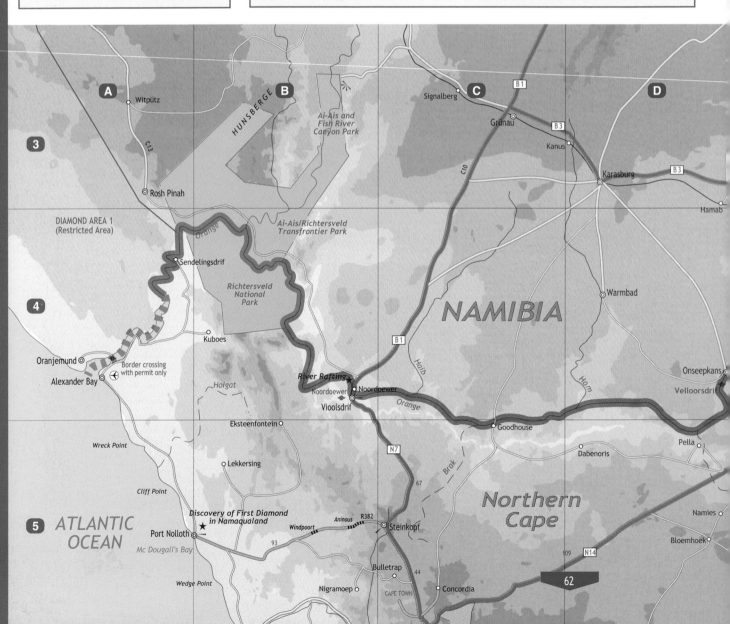

A   No Entry or Exit

B

C   76

D

Tshabong

McCarthy's Rest

1

BOTSWANA

Middelputs

Aansluit

Van Zylsrus

62

82

R31

Rietfontein   Rietfontein

Aroab

Hakskeenpan

Gemsbok

Koppieskraalpan

Witdraai

Andriesvale

Askham

Staansaam

Molopo

Kuruman

196

Sonstraal   116

2

Vredeshoop

Uitsakpan

R31

Noenieput

Cramond

Ontmoeting

KORANNABERG

1550 m

Obobogorab

Koopan Suid

Gaansvlei South

Noenieput

Abiekwasputs

195

Northern Cape

70

Moeswal

3

Langkloof

Vrouenspan

Bokhara

Harrisdale

Swartmodder

Gelukspruit

Grondneus

R360

189

Vroeggedeel

Nakop

Ariamsvlei

Nakop

Langklip

R32   132

N10

Lutzputz

Spitskop NR

BLYDEVERWACHT PLATO

Augrabies Falls National Park

Upington

Karos

Dagbreek

N14

N10

1682 m

4

LANGBERGE

Manie Maritz Fort★

Augrabies Falls

Galab

Orange

River Rafting

Augrabies

Marchand

35

Alheit

Kakamas

Keimoes

N14

Kanoneiland

R359

Neilersdrif

Louisvale

52

Grootdrink

Kalkwerf

120

Wegdraai

R64   Volop

113

Boegoeberg Dam

Bladgrond

N14

Nabies

Kleinbegin

Groblershoop

Orange

SPRINGBOK

R358

112

Hartebeest

Sout

96

R27

Koegrabie

50

Pofadder

Putsonderwater

R383

R383

Koegas

Westerberg

Bossiekom

Tuins

Kenhardt

108

Marydale

ASBESBERGE

5

Geelvloer

Karlvloer

Rootberg Dam

63

62

N10

Fransenhof

R361

Kimberley and Bloemfontein

These neighbouring towns, the capitals of the Northern Cape and Free State provinces respectively, are situated on the high interior plateau. Both offer fine museums and sandstone buildings of historical interest and are surrounded by nature reserves and dams.

Above: *The statue of Christiaan Rudolph de Wet stands in front of Bloemfontein's Fourth Raadsaal, the last government seat of the old Republic.*
Below: *The Kimberley Mine Museum portrays life on the diamond fields more than a century ago.*

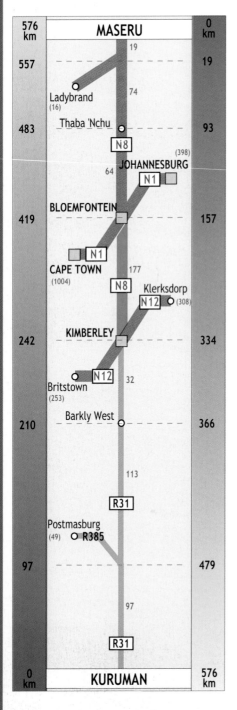

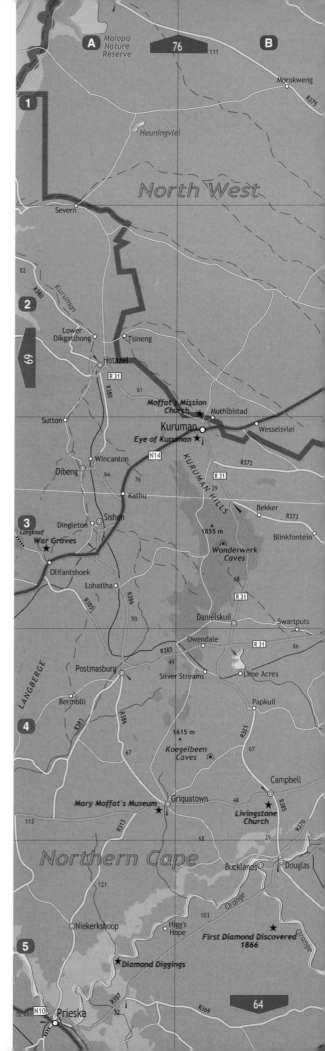

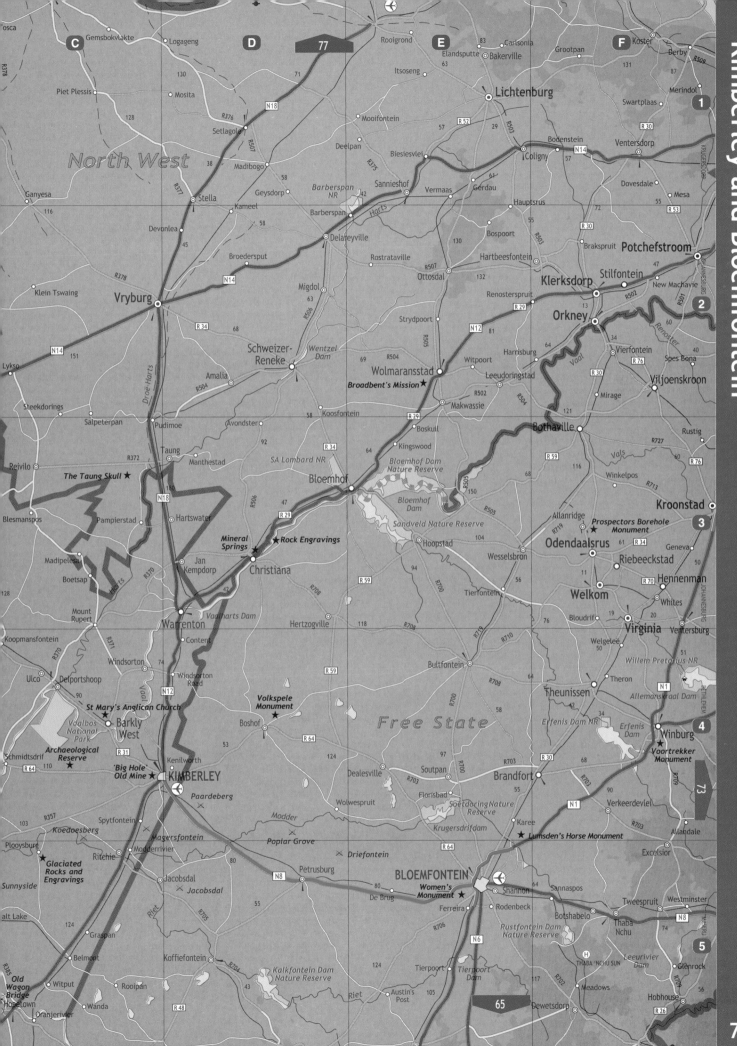

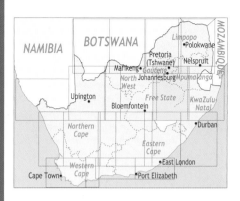

Northeastern Free State

Though much of the Free State consists of flat, treeless grassland plain, the eastern and southern parts are scenically enchanting, rising in a series of picturesquely weathered sandstone hills, and culminating in the high Maluti Mountains of Lesotho in the east. The countryside is at its most spectacular, perhaps, in the Golden Gate Highlands National Park. This is a fertile region, kind to the growers of maize and wheat, sunflowers, fruit (notably cherries) and vegetables. To the north, around Welkom, there are rich deposits of gold.

MAIN ATTRACTIONS

Golden Gate Highlands National Park: south of Bethlehem; sandstone ridges sculpted by the elements; see antelope and over 160 bird species.

Vaal River: border between the Free State and Gauteng; good boating and fishing, especially on the Vaal Dam.

Africa's Best: good game-viewing, including white rhino and buffalo, near Ventersburg; tel: (057) 652-2200.

Pretoriuskloof Bird Sanctuary: near Bethlehem; tel: (058) 303-2211.

Bushman paintings: in the Phuthaditjhaba area, close to Lesotho.

Below: Travellers are often greeted by large fields of glorious golden yellow sunflowers along the Free State roads. These constitute a major crop in the region which has rich soil, despite relatively poor rainfall and very little surface water.

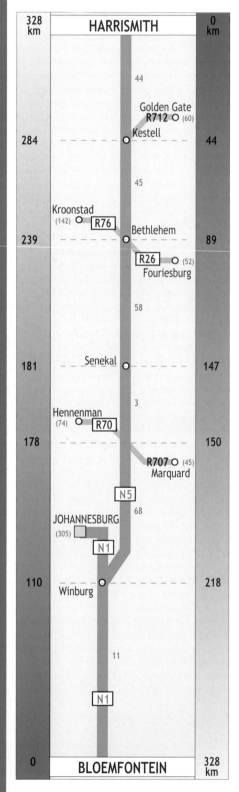

Northern KwaZulu-Natal

*T*he midlands and northern parts of KwaZulu-Natal, overlooked by the Drakensberg massif to the west, are noted for their rolling green hills, rich farmlands, charming country towns — and for their place in the military annals. For much of the 1800s this region served as an immense battleground as three nations fought bitterly for mastery of the land. Closer to the coast lie the splendours of the Greater St Lucia Wetland Park and some of Africa's very finest wildlife reserves. The seaboard is popular among fisherman and boating enthusiasts; offshore lie the world's southernmost coral reefs, a magnet for scuba divers.

324 km	EMPANGENI	0 km
	46	
	R34	
	Gingindlovu (51)	
	R66	
278	Nkwalini	46
	R66	
	27	
	uLundi (53)	
	R66	
251	Melmoth	73
	93	
	R68	
158	Silutshana	166
	72	
	Vryheid (67)	
	R33	
86		238
	2	
84	Dundee	240
	26	
	R68	
	Newcastle (42)	
58		266
	58	
	N11	
0 km	LADYSMITH	324 km

Above: *The Itala Game Reserve, a 30,000ha (74,000-acre) wildlife sanctuary located along the lush banks of the Pongola River, is a haven for the white, or square-lipped, rhino, a highly endangered species. The term 'white' derives from the Afrikaans word 'wyd' (wide) describing the broad, squarish mouth of this mammal.*

MAIN ATTRACTIONS

Howick Falls: outside of Howick, the Mgeni River plunges some 100m (328ft) into a rock pool.

Hluhluwe and iMfolozi Game Reserves: the oldest of South Africa's wildlife sanctuaries, these parks sustain a great number of animals and some 400 species of bird. Tel: (035) 562-0848 / 550-8476.

Itala Game Reserve: home to some 70 species of mammal, among them both white and black rhino, zebra, giraffe, elephant, brown hyena and various antelope. Beautiful Ntshondwe rest camp is just one accommodation alternative that is available here. Tel: (034) 983-2540.

Phinda Resource Reserve: an upmarket ecotourist venture that shares its resources with the local communities, while providing the visitor with an exhilarating wilderness experience. Tel: (035) 562-0271.

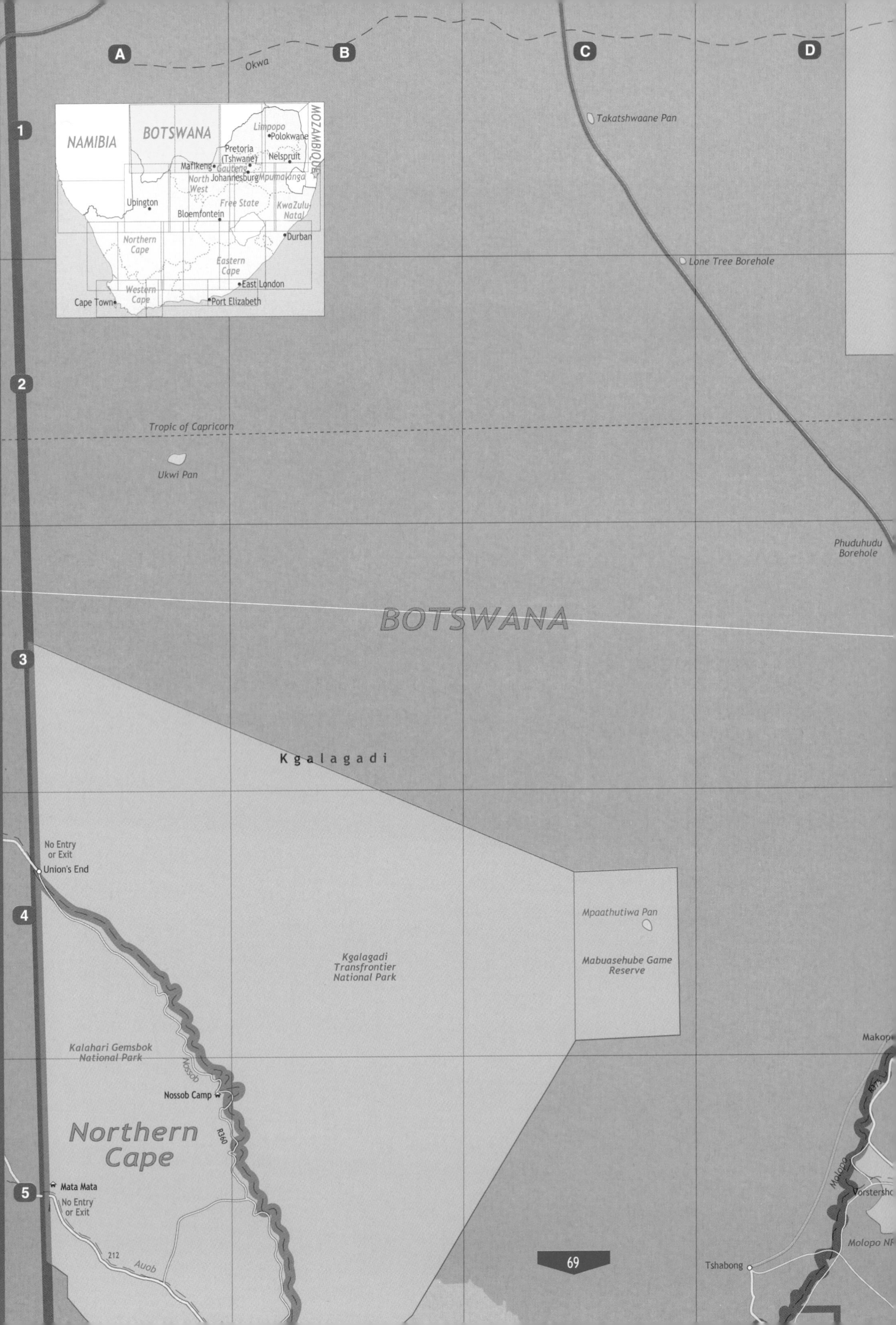

A   B   C   D

Okwa

NAMIBIA   BOTSWANA

Limpopo
•Polokwane

Pretoria
(Tshwane)   Nelspruit

Mafikeng•   •Gauteng

North   Johannesburg•Mpumalanga
West

Free State   KwaZulu-
Natal

Upington•

Bloemfontein•

•Durban

Northern
Cape

Eastern
Cape

Western   •East London
Cape

Cape Town•   •Port Elizabeth

MOZAMBIQUE

1

Takatshwaane Pan

2

Tropic of Capricorn

Lone Tree Borehole

Ukwi Pan

Phuduhudu
Borehole

BOTSWANA

3

Kgalagadi

No Entry
or Exit

Union's End

Mpaathutiwa Pan

4

Kgalagadi
Transfrontier
National Park

Mabuasehube Game
Reserve

Makop

Kalahari Gemsbok
National Park

Nossob

Nossob Camp

R360

Molopo

Northern
Cape

Mata Mata

5

No Entry
or Exit

Vorstersho

212   Auob

69

Tshabong

Molopo NP

R75

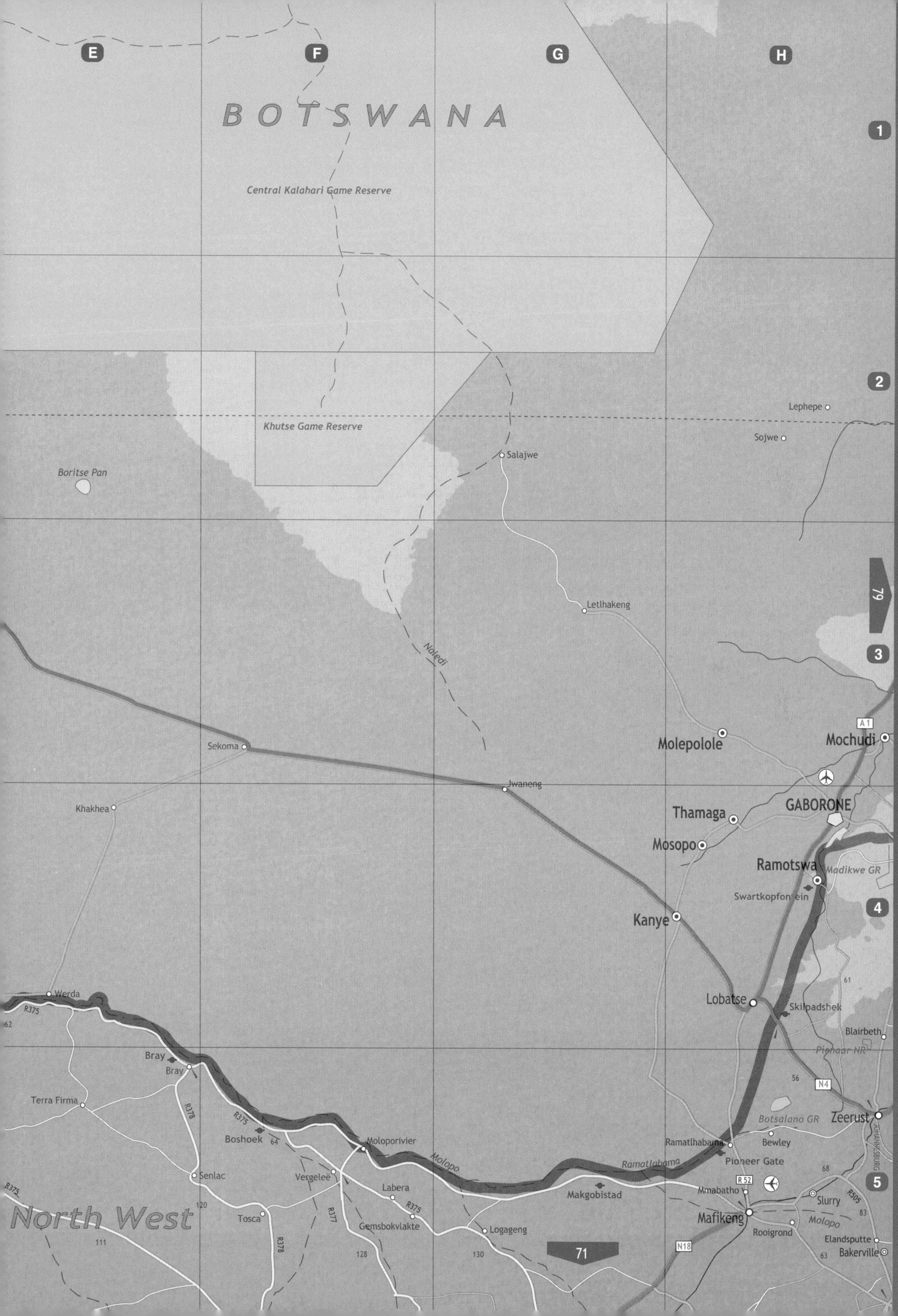

E   F   G   H

1

B O T S W A N A

Central Kalahari Game Reserve

2

Lephepe

Sojwe

Khutse Game Reserve

Salajwe

Boritse Pan

79

Letlhakeng

3

Naledi

A1

Molepolole   Mochudi

Sekoma

Jwaneng   GABORONE

Khakhea   Thamaga

Mosopo

Ramotswa   Madikwe GR

Swartkopfontein

4

Kanye

61

Werda   Lobatse

R375   Skilpadshek

62   Blairbeth

Pilnaar NR

Bray

Bray   56   N4

Terra Firma   Botsalano GR   Zeerust

R378   R375

Boshoek   64   Moloporivier   Ramatlhabama   Bewley

Senlac   Vergelee   Ramatlabama   Pioneer Gate

R375   Labera   Molopo   Makgobistad   Mmabatho   R52   68   Slurry   5

North West   120   R377   Malopo   83

Tosca   R378   Gemsbokvlakte   R375   Mafikeng   Molopo   R305

128   130   Logageng   71   Rooigrond   Elandsputte

111   N18   63   Bakerville

North West and Limpopo

*T*he North West province is a vast, hot, flattish region of bushveld and thorn, of lonely farmsteads, of fields of sunflowers, groundnuts, tobacco, and citrus, and of villages that sleep soundly in the sun. This is one of the great granaries of southern Africa, with endless fields of maize stretching out to the far horizon. Limpopo, which stretches up the lovely Waterberg and Soutpansberg ranges to the Limpopo River valley, is also largely farming country but more densely populated; its principal centre and capital is the pleasant town of Polokwane.

Route chart (km):

	BEIT BRIDGE	
492 km		0 km
476	Musina (16)	16
384	Makhado (92) N1	108
267	Tzaneen R71 (95) (117) / Polokwane	225
210	Zebediela R518 (42) / Mokopane (57)	282
159	Roedtan N11 (39) / Mookgophong (51)	333
101	Bela-Bela (3) R516 (58)	391
0 km	PRETORIA (TSHWANE) (101) N1	492 km

TRAVEL TIPS

All national roads in this area are tarred and generally in excellent condition; most of the secondary roads are gravelled and reasonably well maintained.

The stretch of road between Bela-Bela and Polokwane can get very busy over the Easter weekend. Holiday-makers travelling to the towns and game reserves of the Lowveld join a cavalcade of taxis and buses ferrying worshippers of the ZCC (Zion Christian Church) to their destination, Moria, near Polokwane. Traffic is congested and extreme caution is advised.

MAIN ATTRACTIONS

Sun City and Palace of the Lost City: luxury hotel-casino complex of pure innovation and fantasy.
Pilanesberg Game Reserve: great expanse of wildlife-rich habitat.
Bela-Bela: renowned for its curative springs; the Hydro Spa is of world standard.
Polokwane: principal town of Limpopo; nearby are the **Percy Fyfe Nature Reserve**, where several antelope species may be seen, and the interesting **Bakone Malapa Open-air Museum**, with traditional *kraal* and handicrafts.

Below: The natural springs at Bela-Bela are not the only attraction at this world-class spa resort.

A   B   C   D

1
2
3
4
5

Serowe
Palapye
Mahalapye
Makwate
Parr's Halt
Stockpoort
Mosomane
Spanwerk
Rooibokkraal
Mochudi
Maricosdraai
Sikwane
Derdepoort
Opfontein
Kaya se Put
Zwingli
Madikwe GR
Ganskuil
Nietverdiend
Silkaatskop
Mabeskraal
Straatsdrif
Mabaalstad
Kramellenboog Dam
Skuinsdrif
Marico Bosveld NR
rust
Groot-Marico
Rusverby
Swartruggens
Millvale
Rustenburg
Mabaalstad
Koster
Carlsonia
Grootpan
Wondermere
Derby

BOTSWANA

Tropic of Capricorn

Limpopo
Ngotwane
Matlabas
Crocodile
Mokolo

Lephalale
Afguns
Elmeston
Rooibosbult
Sentrum
Matlabas
Marakele NP
Ben Alberts NR
2085 m
Rankin's
WATERBERGE
Oostermoed
Thabazimbi
Dwaalboom
1499 m
WITFONTEINRANT
Middelwit
Rooiberg
Koedoeskop
Leeuport
Northam
Bier
Mabula
Assen
Atlanta
Klipvoor Dam
Moretele
Borakalalo Game Reserve
Vaalkop Dam
Pilanesberg
1687 m
Pilanesberg Game Reserve
Mogwase
Sun City/Lost City
Beestekraal
Roodekoplies Dam
Paul Kruger's Cottage
Bospoort Dam
Pansdrif
Marikana
Brits
Syringa Tree Stump
Hartbeespoort
Kosmos
Skeerpoort
Magaliesburg Natural Area
MAGALIESBERG
Soutpan
Ga-Rankuwa
Mabopane
Temba
Babelegi
Hammanskraal
Radium

Sherwood Ranch
Groblersbrug
Martin's Drift
Tom Burke
Beauty
75
R572
Monte Christo
Oranjefontein
R572
R510
Ons Hoop
Villa Nora
56
Mokolo Dam
Mokolo Dam NR
R510
Hermanusdorings
R517
41
Vaalwater
Klein-Sand
Alma
48
Mineral Springs
Vanalphensvlei
Haakdoring
Palala
HANGLIPBERGE
Doorndraai Dam NR
Mookgophong
R519
R520
Crecy
Roedtan
R519
82
Modimolle
Middelfontein
R516
104
R33
Holme Park
Settlers
R516
Nutfield
R33
Tuinplaas
Siyabuswa
Rust de Winter
Rust de Winter Nature Reserve
Pienaarsrivier
54
N1
Dennilton
Witnek
Kwamhlanga
Verena
R25
Seringkop
Cullinan
Vaalplaas
R544
Bronkhorstspruit
Kromdraai
Witbank
Balmoral

Zanzibar
Koperspruit
Usutu
Platjan
Gregory
R572
125
R572
Maasstroom
Tonash
De Gracht
Swartwater
N11
Marnitz
Tolwe
Blouberg NR
Baltimore
Woudkop
Senwabarana
Steilloopbrug
Limpopo
Janseput
Marken
178
N11
160
Mogalakwena
Limburg
Matlala
Groesbeek
Mokamole
R518
Percy Fyfe NR
Tinmyne
Mahwelereng
Mokopane
Moorddrif Monument
N1
N11
81

Northern Tuli Conservation Area
Reptile Footprints

Lotsane

Palala
Limpopo
Blouberg NR
Glen Alpine Dam
BLOUBERG

Lapalala Wilderness GR

Limpopo

North West

Mpumalanga

Gauteng

PRETORIA (TSHWANE)
Centurion
Erasmia
Rayton
73
R25
116

Hot Mineral Springs
Bela-Bela
R576
R101
R27
R33

Modimolle

A1
A1
N4
49
81
40
88
48
N4
R52
R24
R509
131
R560
R28
R511
59
R509
R513
89
R513
38
11
N4
N1
R573
156
R573
35

N of 96

79

Limpopo and Mpumalanga

The eastern part of this region is dominated by the Great Escarpment, a spectacular compound of forest-mantled mountains, deep ravines, crystal-clear streams and delicate waterfalls. For sheer scenic beauty, few other parts of the country can compare with this imposing range, which rises near Nelspruit and runs to the northeast for some 300km (186 miles). To the east of the escarpment lies the wildlife-rich Lowveld, where the vast Kruger National Park and a host of beautiful private reserves are situated.

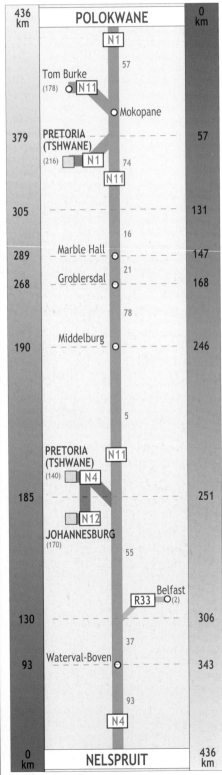

MAIN ATTRACTIONS

Pilgrim's Rest: a living showcase of the early gold-mining days.
Zebediela: South Africa's largest citrus estates are located here.
Polokwane: this is the principal town of Limpopo.
Tzaneen: little town surrounded by waterfalls and forests. Visit nearby **Magoebaskloof** and see the **Modjadjiskloof** realm of the **Modjadji Rain Queen** (source for Sir Rider Haggard's novel *She*) and the impressive cycad forest.
Loskop Dam Game Reserve: wildlife sanctuary around a large dam.
The Sunland Baobab: A 6000-year-old boabab tree near Modjadjiskloof; tel: (015) 309-9039.

Below: *The Blyde River winds its way through the magnificent canyon of the same name.*

TRAVEL TIPS

Most of the roads are tarred, generally in excellent condition and well signposted. The climate is equable, though rainfall during the summer months, from November to February, often occurs in the form of sudden torrential downpours which are accompanied by thunder and lightning. The storms tend to be brief, however, and there are very few days without long hours of sunshine.

A common feature of the escarpment is the occurrence of dense fog patches, and caution is therefore advised. During the 19th and early 20th centuries malaria claimed the lives of many settlers in this area.

The disease is largely under control today, but travellers are strongly advised to take precautionary measures before entering the region.

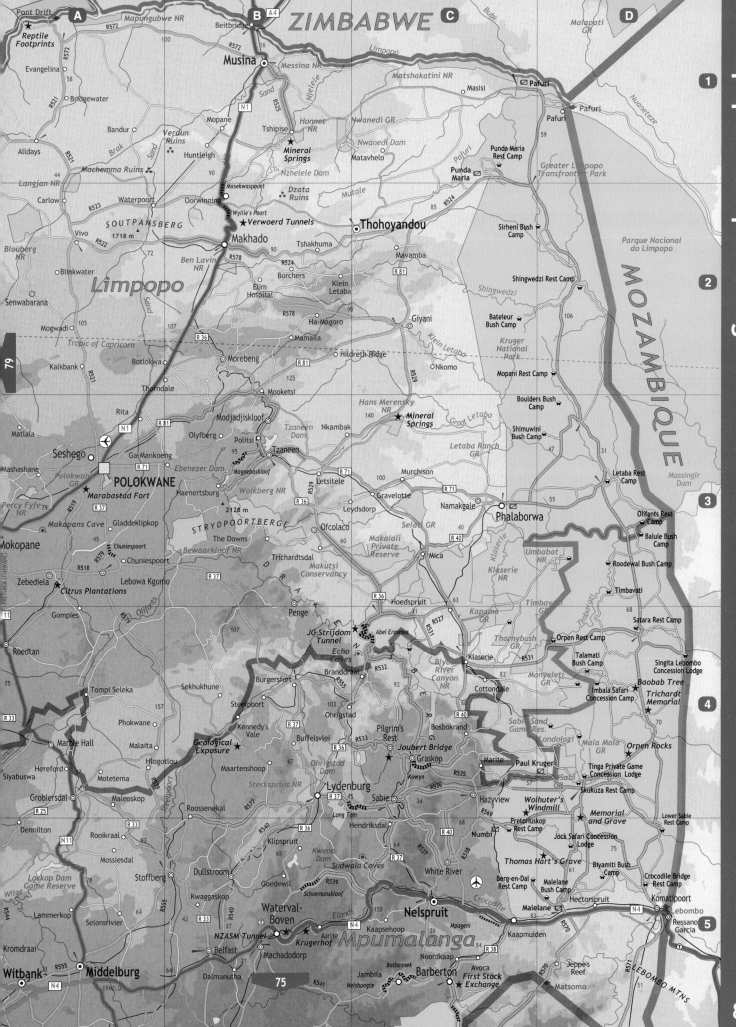

TOURIST AREA AND TEXT INDEX

Note: Numbers in **bold** denote photographs

82

MAIN MAP INDEX

Place	Grid	Pg	Place	Grid	Pg	Place	Grid	Pg	Place	Grid	Pg
Britstown	B2	64	Clanville	B3	66	De Doorns	C1	60	Dysselsdorp	A4	60
Broedersput	D2	71	Clanwilliam	D4	63	De Gracht	D1	79	East London	G4	61
Bronkhorstspruit	C1	73	Clarens	B4	73	De Hoek	D5	63	Eastpoort	E5	65
Brooks Nek	D2	66	Clarkebury	C4	66	De Hoop	A4	60	Edenburg	E1	65
Bruintjieshoogte	E5	65	Clarkson	C5	60	De Klerk	B3	64	Edendale	A1	67
Bucklands	B5	70	Clewer	C1	73	De Rust	A4	60	Edenville	B3	73
Buffelsdrif	B5	60	Clifford	B3	66	Dealesville	E4	71	Eendekuil	D5	63
Buffelsvlei	B4	81	Clocolan	A4	73	Deelfontein	C3	65	Eksteenfontein	B5	68
Bulletrap	B1	62	Coalville	C1	73	Deelpan	E1	71	Elands Height	C2	66
Bultfontein	E4	71	Coega	E5	61	Delareyville	D2	71	Elandsbaai	C4	62
Bulwer	A1	67	Coerney	E4	61	Delmas	C1	73	Elandsdrift	E4	65
Buntingville	D4	66	Coffee Bay	D4	66	Delportshoop	C4	71	Elandskraal	A4	75
Burgersdorp	F3	65	Cofimvaba	B4	66	Demistkraal	D5	60	Elandslaagte	D4	73
Burgersfort	B4	81	Coghlan	C4	66	Deneysville	B2	73	Elandsputte	E1	71
Burgervilleweg	C2	65	Colchester	E5	61	Dennilton	A5	81	Elgin	B2	60
Butterworth	C4	66	Colenso	D4	73	Derby	B5	79	Elim	C3	60
Cala	B3	66	Colesberg	D2	65	Derdepoort	A4	79	Elim Hospital	B2	81
Cala Road	B3	66	Coleskeplaas	C5	60	Despatch	D5	60	Elliot	B3	66
Caledon	C3	60	Coligny	E1	71	Devon	C1	73	Elliotdale	C4	66
Calitzdorp	E2	61	Committees	F4	61	Devonlea	D2	71	Elmeston	C3	79
Calvert	B3	75	Commondale	B3	75	Dewetsdorp	F1	65	Eloff	C1	73
Calvinia	E3	63	Concordia	C5	68	Dibeng	A3	70	eMangusi	D2	75
Cambria	C5	60	Content	D4	71	Die Bos	E4	63	eMpangeni	C5	75
Cameron Glen	E4	65	Conway	E4	65	Die Dam	C3	60	eNtumeni	B5	75
Campbell	B4	70	Cookhouse	E5	65	Die Vlug	B5	60	Erasmia	B1	73
Candover	C3	75	Copperton	A1	64	Diemansputs	G1	63	Ermelo	D2	73
Cape St Francis	D5	60	Cornelia	C2	73	Dieput	C2	65	eShowe	B5	75
Cape Town	B2	60	Cottondale	C4	81	Dingleton	A3	70	Estcourt	D5	73
Carletonville	B1	73	Cradock	E4	65	Dirkiesdorp	A2	75	Evander	C2	73
Carlisle Bridge	F5	65	Cramond	C2	69	Dlolwana	B4	75	Evangelina	A1	81
Carlsonia	A5	79	Crecy	D4	79	Dohne	B5	66	Evaton	B2	73
Carlton	D3	65	Creighton	A2	67	Donkerpoort	E2	65	Excelsior	F5	71
Carnarvon	A3	64	Cullinan	D5	79	Donnybrook	A2	67	eZibeleni	A4	66
Carolina	A1	75	Dabenoris	D5	68	Dordrecht	B3	66	Fairfield	C3	60
Cathcart	B4	66	Dagbreek	C4	69	Doringbaai	C4	62	Faure	B2	60
Cedarville	D2	66	Daggaboersnek	E5	65	Doringbos	D4	63	Fauresmith	E1	65
Cederberg	D5	63	Daleside	B1	73	Douglas	B5	70	Felixton	C5	75
Centani	C5	66	Dalmanutha	A1	75	Dover	B2	73	Ferreira	E5	71
Centurion	B1	73	Dalton	B1	67	Dovesdale	A1	73	Ficksburg	B4	73
Ceres	C1	60	Daniëlskuil	B3	70	Drennan	E4	65	Firgrove	B2	60
Chalumna	G4	61	Danielsrus	B3	73	Driefontein	D4	73	Fish Hoek	B2	60
Charl Cilliers	C2	73	Dannhauser	A3	75	Droërivier	A4	64	Flagstaff	D3	66
Charlestown	D3	73	Darling	B1	60	Dullstroom	B5	81	Florisbad	E4	71
Chieveley	D5	73	Darnall	B5	75	Dundee	A4	75	Fochville	A2	73
Chintsa	C5	66	Daskop	A5	60	Dupleston	F2	65	Fort Beaufort	F5	65
Chrissiesmeer	A1	75	Dasville	C2	73	Durban	B2	67	Fort Brown	F5	65
Christiana	D3	71	Davel	D2	73	Durbanville	B2	60	Fort Donald	D3	66
Chuniespoort	A3	81	Daveyton	C1	73	Dwaal	D3	65	Fort Hare	F4	61
Churchhaven	A1	60	Dawn	G4	61	Dwaalboom	A4	79	Fort Mistake	D4	73
Cintsa	G4	61	De Aar	C2	65	Dwarskersbos	C5	62	Fort Mtombeni	B5	75
Citrusdal	D5	63	De Brug	E5	71	Dwyka	G5	63	Fouriesburg	B4	73

Place	Grid	Pg	Place	Grid	Pg	Place	Grid	Pg	Place	Grid	Pg
Frankfort	D3	73	Graspan	C5	71	Hauptsrus	E2	71	Hout Bay	B2	60
Franklin	D2	66	Gravelotte	C3	81	Hawston	C3	60	Houtkraal	C2	65
Franschhoek	C2	60	Gregory	D1	79	Hazyview	C4	81	Howick	A5	75
Fransenhof	A1	64	Greylingstad	C2	73	Hectorspruit	D5	81	Humansdorp	D5	60
Fraserburg	G4	63	Greystone	D4	60	Heerenlogement	C4	62	Huntleigh	B1	81
Frere	D5	73	Greyton	C2	60	Heidelberg	B2	73	Hutchinson	B3	64
Ga-Mankoeng	B3	81	Greytown	A5	75	Heilbron	B2	73	Idutywa	C4	66
Gamoep	C1	62	Griquatown	A4	70	Helpmekaar	A4	75	iMpendle	A1	67
Gansbaai	C3	60	Groblersdal	A4	81	Helvetia	F1	65	Impisi	A3	67
Ganskuil	A4	79	Groblershoop	D4	69	Hendriksdal	C5	81	iNanda	B1	67
Ganyesa	C1	71	Groenriviers-mond	B3	62	Hendrina	D1	73	Indwe	B3	66
Ga-Rankuwa	C5	79	Groenvlei	A3	75	Hennenman	F3	71	Infanta	D3	60
Garies	B2	62	Groesbeek	D3	79	Herbertsdale	E2	61	Ingogo	D3	73
Garryowen	B3	66	Grondneus	B3	69	Hereford	A4	81	iNgwavuma	C3	75
Geluksburg	D4	73	Groot-Brakrivier	A5	60	Hermanus	C3	60	iSipingo	B2	67
Gelukspruit	B3	69	Grootdrif	D3	63	Hermanusdorings	C3	79	Iswepe	A2	75
Gemsbokvlakte	F5	77	Grootdrink	C4	69	Herold	A5	60	Itsoseng	E1	71
Gemvale	D3	66	Groot-Jongensfontein	E3	61	Herolds Bay	A5	60	iXopo	A2	67
Genadendal	C2	60	Grootkraal	A4	60	Herschel	B2	66	Jacobsdal	C5	71
Geneva	F3	71	Groot-Marico	A5	79	Hertzogville	D3	71	Jagersfontein	E1	65
George	A5	60	Grootmis	A1	62	Het Kruis	D5	63	Jaght Drift	F1	63
Gerdau	E1	71	Grootpan	A5	79	Heuningspruit	A3	73	Jambila	C5	81
Germiston	B1	73	Grootspruit	A3	75	Heydon	D3	65	Jamestown	F3	65
Geysdorp	D1	71	Grootvlei	C2	73	Hibberdene	B2	67	Jammerdrif	A1	66
Giesenskraal	B2	64	Groutville	C1	67	Higg's Hope	A5	70	Jan Kempdorp	D3	71
Gilead	D3	79	Gumtree	A4	73	Highflats	A2	67	Jansenville	D4	60
Gingindlovu	B5	75	Haakdoring	D3	79	Hilandale	D1	60	Janseput	C2	79
Giyani	C2	81	Haarlem	B5	60	Hildreth Ridge	B2	81	Jeffreys Bay	D5	60
Gladdeklipkop	A3	81	Haenertsburg	B3	81	Hillandale	F5	63	Jeppe's Reef	D5	81
Glencoe	A4	75	Haga-Haga	C5	66	Hilton	A1	67	Joel's Drift	B4	73
Glenconnor	D4	60	Halcyon Drift	C3	66	Himeville	D1	66	Johannesburg	B1	73
Glenmore Beach	A3	67	Halfweg	E2	63	Hlabisa	C4	75	Joubertina	C5	60
Glenrock	F5	71	Ha-Magoro	B2	81	Hlobane	B3	75	Jozini	C3	75
Gloria	D1	73	Hamburg	G4	61	Hlogotlou	A4	81	Kaapmuiden	C5	81
Glückstadt	B4	75	Hammanskraal	C5	79	Hluhluwe	C4	75	Kaapsehoop	C5	81
Goedemoed	F2	65	Hammarsdale	B1	67	Hobeni	D4	66	Kakamas	B4	69
Goedewil	B5	81	Hankey	D5	60	Hobhouse	F5	71	Kalbaskraal	B2	60
Golela	C3	75	Hanover Road	D3	65	Hoedspruit	C4	81	Kalkbank	A2	81
Gompies	A4	81	Hanover	D3	65	Hofmeyr	E3	65	Kalkwerf	C4	69
Gonubie	G4	61	Hantam	D3	63	Hogsback	A5	66	Kameel	D2	71
Goodhouse	C5	68	Harding	A2	67	Holbank	A2	75	Kamiesberg	C2	62
Gordon's Bay	B2	60	Harrisburg	F2	71	Holme Park	D4	79	Kamieskroon	B2	62
Gouda	B1	60	Harrisdale	B3	69	Holmedene	C2	73	Kammiebos	C5	60
Gouritsmond	E3	61	Harrismith	C4	73	Hondefontein	G4	63	Kanoneiland	C4	69
Graaff-Reinet	D4	65	Hartbeesfontein	F2	71	Hondeklipbaai	A2	62	Karatara	B5	60
Graafwater	C4	62	Hartbeespoort	C5	79	Hoopstad	E3	71	Karee	E4	71
Grabouw	B2	60	Hartebeeskop	B1	75	Hopefield	B1	60	Kareeboschkolk	E1	63
Grahamstown	F4	61	Hartswater	D3	71	Hopetown	C1	65	Kareedouw	C5	60
Granaatboskolk	E1	63	Hattingspruit	A4	75	Hotagterklip	C3	60	Karkams	B2	62
Graskop	C4	81				Hotazel	A2	70	Karos	C4	69
Grasmere	B1	73				Hottentotskloof	C1	60	Kasouga	F5	61

Name	Grid	Pg	Name	Grid	Pg	Name	Grid	Pg	Name	Grid	Pg
Kathu	A3	70	Komaggas	B1	62	L'Agulhas	D3	60	Luckhoff	D1	65
Kaya se Put	A4	79	Komatipoort	D5	81	Lahlangubo	C3	66	Lundin's Nek	B2	66
Keate's Drift	A5	75	Komga	B5	66	Laingsburg	D1	60	Luneberg	A3	75
Kei Mouth	C5	66	Komkans	C3	62	Lambert's Bay	C4	62	Lusikisiki	D3	66
Kei Road	B5	66	Kommandokraal	B5	64	Lammerkop	A5	81	Luttig	A5	64
Keimoes	B4	69	Kommetjie	B2	60	Landplaas	C3	62	Lutzputz	B4	69
Keiskammahoek	B5	66	Kommissiepoort	A5	73	Langberg	E2	61	Lutzville	C4	62
Kempton Park	B1	73	Koopan Suid	B2	69	Langdon	C4	66	Lydenburg	B4	81
Kendal	C1	73	Koopmansfontein	C4	71	Langebaan	A1	60	Lykso	C2	71
Kendrew	D5	65	Koosfontein	D2	71	Langholm	F4	61	Maartenshoop	B4	81
Kenhardt	C5	69	Kootjieskolk	E3	63	Langklip	B4	69	Maasstroom	D1	79
Kenilworth	D4	71	Koperspruit	D1	79	Leandra	C1	73	Mabaalstad	A5	79
Kennedy's Vale	B4	81	Koppies	A2	73	Lebowa Kgomo	A3	81	Mabeskraal	A4	79
Kenton on Sea	F5	61	Koringberg	B1	60	Leeudoringstad	E2	71	Mabopane	C5	79
Kestell	C4	73	Koringplaas	F5	63	Leeu-Gamka	G5	63	Mabula	C4	79
Kidd's Beach	G4	61	Kosmos	C5	79	Leeuport	C4	79	Machadodorp	B5	81
Kimberley	C4	71	Koster	B5	79	Lehlohonolo	D2	66	Macleantown	B5	66
King William's Town	B5	66	Kotzesrus	B3	62	Leipoldtville	C4	62	Maclear	C3	66
Kingsburgh	B2	67	Koukraal	F2	65	Lekfontein	F5	65	Madadeni	A3	75
Kingscote	D2	66	Koup	E1	61	Lekkersing	B5	68	Madibogo	D1	71
Kingsley	A3	75	Koutjie	A5	60	Lemoenshoek	D2	60	Madipelesa	C3	71
Kingswood	E3	71	Kraaifontein	B2	60	Lephalale	C2	79	Mafeteng	B1	66
Kinirapoort	C2	66	Kraaldorings	E1	61	Letjiesbos	A5	64	Mafikeng	H5	77
Kinross	C1	73	Kraankuil	C1	65	Letsitele	B3	81	Mafube	D2	66
Kirkwood	D4	60	Kransfontein	C4	73	Leydsdorp	B3	81	Magaliesburg	A1	73
Klaarstroom	A4	60	Kranskop	A5	75	Libertas	B4	73	Magudu	C3	75
Klaserie	C4	81	Kriel	C1	73	Libode	D3	66	Mahlabatini	B4	75
Klawer	C4	62	Kromdraai	A5	81	Lichtenburg	E1	71	Mahlangasi	C3	75
Klein Drakenstein	B2	60	Kroonstad	A3	73	Lidgetton	A1	67	Mahwelereng	D3	79
Klein Letaba	B2	81	Krugers	E1	65	Limburg	D3	79	Maizefield	D2	73
Klein Tswaing	C2	71	Krugersdorp	B1	73	Lime Acres	B4	70	Makhado	B2	81
Kleinbegin	C4	69	Kruidfontein	G5	63	Lindeshof	C2	60	Makwassie	E2	71
Kleinmond	B3	60	Kruisfontein	D5	60	Lindley	B3	73	Malaita	A4	81
Kleinpoort	D4	60	Kruisrivier	E1	61	Llandudno	B2	60	Maleoskop	A4	81
Kleinsee	A1	62	Kuboes	B4	68	Loch Vaal	B2	73	Malgas	D3	60
Klerksdorp	F2	71	Kuilsriver	B2	60	Lochiel	B1	75	Malmesbury	B2	60
Klerkskraal	A1	73	Ku-Mayima	C3	66	Loerie	D5	60	Mamaila	B2	81
Klipdale	C3	60	Kuruman	B3	70	Loeriesfontein	D3	63	Mamre	B2	60
Klipfontein	D1	73	KwaDweshula	A2	67	Lofter	E2	65	Mandini	B5	75
Klipplaat	C5	65	Kwaggaskop	B5	81	Logageng	G5	77	Mangeni	A4	75
Kliprand	C2	62	KwaMashu	B1	67	Lohatlha	A3	70	Manthestad	D3	71
Klipspruit	B5	81	KwaMbonambi	C4	75	Long Hope	E5	65	Mantsonyane	C1	66
Knapdaar	F2	65	Kwamhlanga	D5	79	Loskop	D5	73	Mapumulo	B5	75
Knysna	B5	60	Kylemore	B2	60	Lothair	A1	75	Marakabei	C1	66
Koedoeskop	B4	79	Laaiplek	A1	60	Louisvale	C4	69	Marble Hall	A4	81
Koegas	D5	69	Labera	F5	77	Louterwater	C5	60	Marburg	A3	67
Koegrabie	C5	69	Ladismith	E1	61	Louwsburg	B3	75	Marchand	B4	69
Koffiefontein	D1	65	Lady Frere	B4	66	Lower Dikgatlhong	A2	70	Margate	A3	67
Koingnaas	A2	62	Lady Grey	B2	66	Lower Pitseng	C2	66	Maricosdraai	A3	79
Kokstad	D2	66	Ladybrand	A5	73	Loxton	A3	64	Marikana	B5	79
			Ladysmith	D4	73				Marite	C4	81

Place	Grid	No.	Place	Grid	No.
Marken	D2	79	Modderrivier	C5	71
Marnitz	C2	79	Modimolle	C4	79
Marquard	A4	73	Modjadjiskloof	B3	81
Martin's Drift	C2	79	Moeswal	D3	69
Marydale	D5	69	Mogalakwena	D3	79
Mashashane	A3	81	Mogwadi	A2	81
Masisi	C1	81	Mogwase	B4	79
Matatiele	D2	66	Mohales Hoek	B2	66
Matavhelo	C1	81	Mokamole	D3	79
Matjiesfontein	D1	60	Mokopane	D3	79
Matjiesrivier	A4	60	Moloporivier	F5	77
Matlabas	B3	79	Molteno	F3	65
Matlala	A3	81	Mont Pelaan	D3	73
Matroosberg	C1	60	Montagu	D2	60
Mavamba	C2	81	Monte Christo	C2	79
Mazeppa Bay	C5	66	Mooi River	D5	73
Mbashe Bridge	C4	66	Mooifontein	E1	71
Mbazwana	D3	75	Mooketsi	B2	81
Mbotyi	A3	67	Mookgophong	D4	79
McGregor	C2	60	Moordkuil	C2	60
Mdantsane	G4	61	Moorreesburg	B1	60
Meadows	A1	66	Mopane	B1	81
Melkbosstrand	B2	60	Morebeng	B2	81
Melmoth	B4	75	Morgan's Bay	C5	66
Meltonwold	A3	64	Morgenzon	D2	73
Memel	D3	73	Morokweng	A2	70
Merindol	F1	71	Morristown	B3	66
Merriman	C3	65	Mortimer	E4	65
Merweville	G5	63	Moshesh's Ford	B3	66
Mesa	F1	71	Mosita	D1	71
Mesklip	B1	62	Mossel Bay	A5	60
Meyerton	B2	73	Mossiesdal	A5	81
Meyerville	C2	73	Motetema	A4	81
Mgwali	B5	66	Mothibistad	B2	70
Mica	C3	81	Mount Ayliff	D3	66
Middelburg	A5	81	Mount Fletcher	C2	66
Middelburg	D3	65	Mount Frere	D3	66
Middelfontein	D4	79	Mount Rupert	C3	71
Middelpos	E4	63	Mount Stewart	D5	65
Middelwit	B4	79	Moyeni	B2	66
Middleton	E5	65	Mpemvana	A3	75
Midrand	B1	73	Mpethu	C5	66
Migdol	D2	71	Mphaki	C2	66
Miller	C5	65	Mpolweni	A5	75
Millvale	B5	79	Mpumalanga	B1	67
Milnerton	B2	60	Mt Moorosi	C2	66
Mirage	F2	71	Mthatha	D3	66
Misgund	B5	60	Mtkonjeneni	B4	75
Mkambati	A3	67	Mtubatuba	C4	75
Mkhuze	C3	75	Mtunzini	C5	75
Mmabatho	H5	77	Mtwalume	B2	67

Place	Grid	No.	Place	Grid	No.
Muden	A5	75	Noordhoek	B2	60
Muizenberg	B2	60	Noordkaap	C5	81
Munster	A3	67	Noordkuil	C5	62
Munyu	C4	66	Normandien	D3	73
Murchison	C3	81	Northam	B4	79
Murraysburg	C4	65	Norvalspont	E2	65
Musina	B1	81	Nottingham Road	D5	73
Mynfontein	C3	65	Noupoort	D3	65
Nababeep	B1	62	Nqabarha	D4	66
Nabies	A4	69	Nqutu	A4	75
Nakop	A3	69	Ntabamhlope	D5	73
Namakgale	C3	81	Ntabankulu	D3	66
Namies	D5	68	Ntibane	C3	66
Napier	C3	60	Ntseshe	C4	66
Nariep	B3	62	Ntshilini	D4	66
Nature's Valley	B5	60	Ntywenke	C3	66
Ncanara	E5	61	Nutfield	D4	79
Ndumo	C2	75	Nuwerus	C3	62
Ndundulu	B4	75	Nuy	C2	60
Ndwedwe	B1	67	Nyokana	C4	66
Neilersdrif	C4	69	Oatlands	C5	65
Nelspoort	B4	64	Obobogorab	A2	69
Nelspruit	C5	81	Odendaalsrus	F3	71
New Amalfi	D2	66	Ofcolaco	B3	81
New England	B3	66	Ogies	C1	73
New Hanover	B1	67	Ohrigstad	B4	81
New Machavie	F2	71	Okiep	B1	62
Newcastle	D3	73	Old Bunting	D4	66
Ngcobo	C4	66	Old Morley	D4	66
Ngobeni	B3	75	Olifantshoek	A3	70
Ngome	B3	75	Olyfberg	B3	81
Ngqamakhwe	C4	66	Omdraaisvlei	B2	64
Ngqeleni	D4	66	Onderstedorings	F2	63
Ngqungqu	C4	66	Ons Hoop	C2	79
Niekerkshoop	A5	70	Ontmoeting	C2	69
Nietverdiend	A4	79	Oorwinning	B2	81
Nieu-Bethesda	D4	65	Oostermoed	B4	79
Nieuwoudtville	D3	63	Orania	D1	65
Nigel	C1	73	Oranjefontein	C2	79
Nigramoep	B5	68	Oranjerivier	C5	71
Nkambak	B3	81	Oranjeville	B2	73
Nkandla	B4	75	Orkney	F2	71
Nkau	C2	66	Osborn	B4	75
Nkomo	C2	81	oSizweni	A3	75
Nkwalini	B4	75	Ottosdal	E2	71
Nobantu	D3	66	Oudtshoorn	A4	60
Nobhokhwe	B4	66	Oukraal	C3	60
Noenieput	A3	69	Ouplaas	D3	60
Noll	B5	60	Oviston	E2	65
Nondweni	A4	75	Owendale	B4	70
Nongoma	B3	75	Oyster Bay	D5	60

Paarl	B2	60	Plettenberg Bay	B5	60	Ramabanta	B1	66	Rooigrond	H5	77
Pacaltsdorp	A5	60	Plooysburg	C5	71	Ramatlhabama	H5	77	Rooikraal	A5	81
Paddock	A3	67	Pniel	B2	60	Ramsgate	A3	67	Rooipan	C5	71
Pafuri	D1	81	Pofadder	A5	69	Randalhurst	B4		Rooiwal	A2	73
Palala	D3	79	Politsi	B3	81	Randburg	B1	73	Roosboom	D4	73
Paleisheuwel	D5	63	Polokwane	A3	81	Randfontein	B1	73	Roossenekal	B4	81
Palmerton	D3	66	Pomeroy	A4	75	Ratelfontein	C4	62	Rorke's Drift	A4	75
Palmietfontein	B2	66	Pongola	C3	75	Rawsonville	C2	60	Rosebank	A2	67
Pampierstad	C3	71	Pools	D5	63	Rayton	D5	79	Rosedene	A4	64
Pampoenpoort	A3	64	Port Alfred	F5	61	Redcliffe	D5	73	Rosendal	B4	73
Panbult	A2	75	Port Beaufort	D3	60	Reddersburg	F1	65	Rosetta	D5	73
Pansdrif	C5	79	Port Edward	A3	67	Redelinghuys	C5	62	Rosmead	D3	65
Papendorp	C4	62	Port Elizabeth	E5	61	Redoubt	A3	67	Rossouw	B3	66
Papiesvlei	C3	60	Port Grosvenor	A3	67	Reebokrand	D1	65	Rostrataville	E2	71
Papkuil	B4	70	Port Nolloth	B5	68	Reitz	B3	73	Rouxpos	E1	61
Park Rynie	B2	67	Port Shepstone	B3	67	Reitzburg	A2	73	Rouxville	A2	66
Parow	B2	60	Port St Johns	D4	66	Reivilo	C3	71	Ruitersbos	E2	61
Parys	A2	73	Porterville	D5	63	Renosterkop	B4	64	Rust de Winter	D4	79
Patensie	D5	60	Post Chalmers	E4	65	Renosterspruit	F2	71	Rust	B1	60
Paternoster	B5	62	Postmasburg	A4	70	Restvale	B4	64	Rustenburg	B5	79
Paterson	E4	61	Potchefstroom	A2	73	Rhodes	C2	66	Rustig	F3	71
Paul Roux	B4	73	Potfontein	C2	65	Richards Bay	C5	75	Rusverby	A5	79
Paulpietersburg	B3	75	Potsdam	G4	61	Richmond	C3	65	Saaifontein	G4	63
Pearly Beach	C3	60	Poupan	C1	65	Riebeeckstad	F3	71	Sabie	C4	81
Pearston	D5	65	Pretoria			Riebeek Kasteel	B1	60	Sada	F4	65
Peddie	F4	61	(Tshwane)	C5	79	Riebeek-Oos	E4	61	Sakrivier	E3	63
Pella	D5	68	Prieska	A5	70	Riebeek-Wes	B1	60	Saldanha	A1	60
Penge	B3	81	Prince Albert	E1	61	Rietbron	B5	64	Salem	F4	61
Perdekop	D2	73	Prince Albert			Rietfontein	A2	69	Salpeterpan	C2	71
Petersburg	D4	65	Road	G5	63	Rietkuil	C3	73	Salt Lake	C5	71
Petrus Steyn	B3	73	Prince Alfred			Rietpoel	C3	60	Salt Rock	C1	67
Petrusburg	D5	71	Hamlet	C1	60	Rietpoort	B3	62	Sand River Valley	D4	73
Petrusville	D1	65	Pringle Bay	B3	60	Rietvlei	A5	75	Sandberg	C4	62
Phalaborwa	C3	81	Priors	E2	65	Rita	A3	81	Sandton	B1	73
Philadelphia	B2	60	Protem	D3	60	Ritchie	C5	71	Sandvlakte	C5	60
Philippolis	E2	65	Pudimoe	C3	71	River View	C4	75	Sannaspos	F5	71
Philippolis Road	E2	65	Puntjie	E3	61	Riversdale	E2	61	Sannieshof	E1	71
Philipstown	D2	65	Putsonderwater	D5	69	Riverside	A2	67	Sasolburg	B2	73
Phokwane	A4	81	Qacha's Nek	D2	66	Riviersonderend	C2	60	Sauer	C5	62
Phuthaditjhaba	C4	73	Qamata	B4	66	Roamer's Rest	C2	66	Scarborough	B2	60
Pienaarsrivier	C4	79	Qholhora Mouth	C5	66	Robert's Drift	C2	73	Scheepersnek	A3	75
Piet Plessis	C1	71	Qhorha Mouth	C5	66	Robertson	C2	60	Schmidtsdrif	C4	71
Piet Retief	B2	75	Qiba	B3	66	Rode	D3	66	Schoombee	E3	65
Pieter Meintjies	D1	60	Qoboqobo	C5	66	Rodenbeck	E5	71	Schweizer-		
Pietermaritzburg	B1	67	Qoqodala	F4	65	Roedtan	A4	81	Reneke	D2	71
Piketberg	D5	63	Qudeni	A4	75	Rondevlei	A5	60	Scottburgh	B2	67
Pilgrim's Rest	C4	81	Queensburgh	B2	67	Roodebank	C2	73	Sea Park	B3	67
Pinetown	B1	67	Queenstown	F4	65	Roodepoort	B1	73	Seaview	D5	60
Platbakkies	C2	62	Quko	C5	66	Rooiberg	C4	79	Secunda	C2	73
Plathuis	D2	60	Qumbu	D3	66	Rooibokkraal	B3	79	Sedgefield	B5	60
Platrand	D2	73	Radium	C4	79	Rooibosbult	B3	79	Seekoegat	A5	64

Name	Grid	Page	Name	Grid	Page	Name	Grid	Page	Name	Grid	Page
Sekhukhune	B4	81	Spanwerk	B3	79	Stutterheim	B5	66	Tombo	D4	66
Selonsrivier	A5	81	Spes Bona	A2	73	Summerstrand	E5	61	Tompi Seleka	A4	81
Sendelingsdrif	A4	68	Spitskopvlei	D4	65	Sun City/			Tonash	D1	79
Senekal	A4	73	Spoegrivier	B2	62	Lost City	B5	79	Tongaat	B1	67
Senlac	E5	77	Spring Valley	F4	65	Sunland	E4	61	Tontelbos	E3	63
Sentrum	B3	79	Springbok	B1	62	Sutherland	F4	63	Tosca	F5	77
Senwabarana	A2	81	Springfontein	E2	65	Sutton	A3	70	Touwsriver	C1	60
Seringkop	D5	79	Springs	C1	73	Suurbraak	D2	60	Trawal	C4	62
Seshego	A3	81	Spytfontein	C4	71	Swaershoek	E5	65	Trichardt	C2	73
Setlagole	D1	71	St Faith's	A2	67	Swartberg	D2	66	Trichardtsdal	B3	81
Settlers	D4	79	St Francis Bay	D5	60	Swartkops	E5	61	Triple Streams	C3	66
Sevenoaks	A5	75	St Helena Bay	C5	62	Swartmodder	B3	69	Trompsburg	E1	65
Severn	A2	70	St Lucia	C4	75	Swartplaas	A1	73	Tsazo	C4	66
Seweweekspoort	E1	61	St Marks	B4	66	Swartputs	B4	70	Tshakhuma	B2	81
Seymour	F5	65	Staansaam	B2	69	Swartruggens	A5	79	Tshani	D4	66
Sezela	B2	67	Stafford's Post	A2	67	Swartwater	C1	79	Tshipise	B1	81
Shaka's Rock	C1	67	Standerton	C2	73	Swellendam	D2	60	Tsineng	A2	70
Shakaskraal	C1	67	Stanford	C3	60	Swempoort	B3	66	Tsitsa Bridge	D3	66
Shannon	E5	71	Stanger	C1	67	Swinburne	C4	73	Tsoelike	D2	66
Sheepmoor	A2	75	Steekdorings	C2	71	Syfergat	A3	66	Tsolo	D3	66
Sheldon	E5	65	Steelpoort	B4	81	Tafelberg	D3	65	Tsomo	B4	66
Sherborne	D3	65	Steilloopbrug	D2	79	Tainton	C5	66	Tugela Ferry	A4	75
Sidwadweni	D3	66	Steilrand	B3	75	Taleni	C4	66	Tugela Mouth	B5	75
Sigoga	D2	66	Steinkopf	C5	68	Tarkastad	F4	65	Tuinplaas	D4	79
Silkaatskop	A4	79	Stella	D1	71	Taung	D3	71	Tulbagh	C1	60
Silutshana	A4	75	Stellenbosch	B2	60	Temba	C5	79	Tunnel	C1	60
Silver Streams	B4	70	Sterkaar	C3	65	Tembisa	B1	73	Tweefontein	E4	63
Simon's Town	B3	60	Sterkspruit	B2	66	Terra Firma	E5	77	Tweeling	C3	73
Sinksabrug	A5	60	Sterkstroom	F3	65	Teviot	E4	65	Tweespruit	F5	71
Sir Lowry's Pass	B2	60	Sterling	G3	63	Teza	C4	75	Tyira	D3	66
Sishen	A3	70	Steynsburg	E3	65	Thaba Chitja	C2	66	Tylden	B4	66
Sittingbourne	B5	66	Steynsrus	A3	73	Thaba 'Nchu	F5	71	Tzaneen	B3	81
Siyabuswa	A4	81	Steytlerville	C4	60	Thaba Tseka	C1	66	Ubombo	C3	75
Skeerpoort	C5	79	Stilfontein	F2	71	Thabazimbi	B4	79	Ugie	C3	66
Skipskop	D3	60	Still Bay East	E3	61	The Crags	B5	60	Uitenhage	D5	60
Skuinsdrif	A5	79	Still Bay West	E3	61	The Downs	B3	81	Uitkyk	C1	62
Slurry	H5	77	Stockpoort	B2	79	The Haven	D4	66	Uitspankraal	D4	63
Smithfield	A2	66	Stoffberg	B5	81	The Heads	B5	60	Ulco	C4	71
Smitskraal	C5	60	Stofvlei	C2	62	The Ranch	A5	75	uLundi	B4	75
Sneeukraal	A4	64	Stompneusbaai	B5	62	Theron	F4	71	uMbogintwini	B2	67
Sodium	B2	64	Stoneyridge	D3	66	Theunissen	F4	71	uMgababa	B2	67
Soebatsfontein	B2	62	Stormberg	F3	65	Thohoyandou	C2	81	uMhlanga	B1	67
Somerset East	E5	65	Stormsrivier	C5	60	Thorndale	A2	81	uMkomaas	B2	67
Somerset West	B2	60	Stormsvlei	D2	60	Thornville	B1	67	uMlazi	B2	67
Somkele	C4	75	Straatsdrif	A4	79	Three Sisters	B4	64	Umtentu	A3	67
Sonstraal	D2	69	Strand	B2	60	Tierfontein	E3	71	uMtentweni	B3	67
Southbroom	A3	67	Strandfontein	C4	62	Tierpoort	F1	65	Umzimkulu	A2	67
Southeyville	B4	66	Struisbaai	D3	60	Tina Bridge	D3	66	uMzinto	B2	67
Southwell	F5	61	Strydenburg	C1	65	Tinmyne	D3	79	Underberg	D1	66
Soutpan	C5	79	Strydpoort	E2	71	Tolwe	D2	79	Uniondale	B5	60
Soweto	B1	73	Studtis	C4	60	Tom Burke	C2	79	Union's End	A4	76

Upington	C4	69	Volksrust	D3	73	Willowvale	C4	66
Usutu	D1	79	Volop	D4	69	Winburg	A4	73
Utrecht	A3	75	Volstruisleegte	B5	64	Wincanton	A3	70
uVongo	A3	67	Vorstershoop	D5	76	Windmeul	B2	60
Vaalplaas	D5	79	Vosburg	B2	64	Windsorton	C4	71
Vaalwater	C3	79	Vrede	C3	73	Windsorton Road	D4	71
Val	C2	73	Vredefort	A2	73	Winkelpos	F3	71
Valsrivier	B4	73	Vredenburg	A1	60	Winterton	D4	73
Van Reenen	D4	73	Vredendal	C4	62	Witbank	D1	73
Van Wyksdorp	E2	61	Vroeggedeel	D3	69	Witdraai	B2	69
Van Wyksvlei	G2	63	Vrouenspan	B3	69	Witkop	A3	66
Van Zylsrus	D2	69	Vryburg	C2	71	Witmos	E5	65
Vanalphensvlei	D3	79	Vryheid	A3	75	Witnek	D5	79
Vanderbijlpark	B2	73	Wagenaarskraal	B4	64	Witpoort	E2	71
Vanderkloof	D1	65	Wakkerstroom	A3	75	Witput	C5	71
Vandyksdrif	D1	73	Wallekraal	B2	62	Witsand	D3	60
Vanrhynsdorp	C4	62	Wanda	C5	71	Wittedrif	B5	60
Vanstadensrus	B1	66	Waqu	B4	66	Witteklip	D5	60
Vant's Drift	A4	75	Warburton	A1	75	Witwater	C2	62
Vegkop	B3	73	Warden	C3	73	Wolmaransstad	E2	71
Velddrif	C5	62	Warmwaterberg	D2	60	Wolseley	C1	60
Ventersburg	A3	73	Warrenton	D3	71	Wolwefontein	D4	60
Ventersdorp	F1	71	Wasbank	A4	75	Wolwehoek	B2	73
Venterskroon	A2	73	Waterford	D5	65	Wolwespruit	D4	71
Venterstad	E2	65	Waterkloof	E2	65	Wonderkop	A3	73
Vereeniging	B2	73	Waterval-Boven	B5	81	Wondermere	A5	79
Verena	D5	79	Wavecrest	C5	66	Woodlands	C5	60
Vergeleë	F5	77	Waverley	B1	75	Wooldridge	F4	61
Verkeerdevlei	F4	71	Weenen	A5	75	Worcester	C2	60
Verkykerskop	C3	73	Wegdraai	D4	69	Woudkop	D2	79
Vermaaklikheid	E3	61	Welgeleë	F4	71	Wuppertal	D4	63
Vermaas	E1	71	Welkom	F3	71	Wyford	D4	73
Verster	B3	64	Wellington	B2	60	Xolobe	B4	66
Verulam	B1	67	Welverdiend	A1	73	Yzerfontein	A1	60
Victoria West	B3	64	Wepener	B1	66	Zaaimansdal	B5	60
Viedgesville	C4	66	Wesley	G4	61	Zastron	B2	66
Vierfontein	F2	71	Wesselsbron	E3	71	Zebediela	A3	81
Viljoensdrif	B2	73	Wesselsvlei	B3	70	Zeerust	A5	79
Viljoenshof	C3	60	Westerberg	D5	69	Zoar	E1	61
Viljoenskroon	A2	73	Westleigh	A3	73	Zunckels	D5	73
Villa Nora	C2	79	Westminster	A5	73	Zwartkop	F2	63
Villiers	C2	73	Westonaria	A1	73	Zwarts	E1	61
Villiersdorp	C2	60	Weza	A2	67	Zwelitsha	G4	61
Vineyard	A3	66	White River	C5	81	Zwingli	A4	79
Vioolsdrif	B4	68	Whites	A3	73			
Virginia	F3	71	Whitmore	C3	66			
Visrivier	E4	65	Whittlesea	A4	66			
Vivo	A2	81	Wiegnaarspoort	B5	64			
Vleesbaai	E3	61	Wilderness	A5	60			
Vleifontein	E1	61	Williston	F3	63			
Vleiland	E1	61	Willowmore	B4	60			